David Lampe
K'zoo
May '94

LITERARY STRUCTURES

Edited by John Gardner

FLAMBOYANT DRAMA

A Study of *The Castle of Perseverance, Mankind,* and *Wisdom*

By Michael R. Kelley
Foreword by John Gardner

Southern Illinois University Press
Carbondale and Edwardsville

FEFFER & SIMONS, INC.
London and Amsterdam

Library of Congress Cataloging in Publication Data

Kelley, Michael R   1940–
    Flamboyant drama.

    Includes index.
        1. Moralities, English—History and criticism.   2. Castle of perseverance
    (Morality play)   3. Mankind (Morality play)   4. Wisdom (Morality play)
    I. Title.
    PR643.M7K4   822'.2'09   78-31237
    ISBN 0-8093-0915-7

FOR OWEN

Contents

Illustrations

Foreword

In the Middle Ages, especially in England, drama was more popular than it had ever been before, even in ancient Greece, or has ever been since, even in Shakespeare's London. Thousands upon thousands of people went to see plays of all kinds—folk plays, masquelike plays, guild plays, and so on. For a long time scholars were baffled by the popularity of medieval theater. Reading the plays' dull poetry, as they thought it, or studying the seemingly clumsy dramatic structure, they shook their heads in puzzlement at the astounding attendance records and the huge sums of money involved in dramatic production.

Then, for one group of plays at least—the guild or "mystery" plays—scholarly opinion began to change. Over the past twenty years, scholars began to see and point out, in one fascinating book after another, how subtly some of the mystery-play poetry worked when taken on its own terms, how ingeniously the plays were in fact constructed, and how fine the theatrical effects must have been. As a result of that work, it no longer seems a mystery that the mystery plays were so well attended. On the contrary, the mystery has come to be that such wonderful entertainments should give way, toward the end of the medieval period, to the seemingly stiff, deadly dull "Macro plays," as they've unfortunately come to be called.

Now Michael Kelley has done for the Macro plays what earlier scholars did for the mysteries: he has pointed out their controlling aesthetic and shown why, in their time and place, they were a joy to see and hear. They were, he shows, a kind of entertainment for which we can find no easy parallels—part opera, part dance, part drama, part circus, and more. For the first time since they vanished from the face of the earth, Professor Kelley makes available, at least to our imagination, the experience of these strange, magnificent celebrations. They represent an art form we will never see again. Now that we know something about how they were done, we can restage the mystery plays; but in a world where even proper staging of Verdi's *Aïda* is financially prohibitive, we can sooner coat the moon with aluminum than mount authentic productions of the plays in this book. No doubt it's just as well. They reflect ideas we no longer believe, a vision and a set of aesthetic presuppositions we can nowadays admire but not love. Professor Kelley's study makes that vision and set of aesthetic presuppositions clear and enables us to read these old texts not as curiosities but as works of art. But his study also does something more: it enables us to glimpse a vanished world, a society which, though part of our heritage, may at times seem as strange to us as Egyptian mechanics or the religious opinions of a whale.

Professor Kelley teaches medieval literature at George Mason University and has published numerous articles in the field. He has also worked, in various capacities, on radio and television programs.

Lanesboro, Pennsylvania   John Gardner
January 1979

Preface

The Castle of Perseverance, Mankind, and *Wisdom* have received little mercy from literary critics. Admittedly, things have improved somewhat since 1792, when the anonymous author of *A New Theatrical Dictionary* (London: S. Bladon, 1792) wrote: "[The period of the mystery plays] one might call the dead sleep of the muses. And when this was over, they did not presently awake, but, in a kind of morning dream, produced the moralities that followed" (p. 384). The improved critical attitude hasn't been overwhelming, and even now it's almost impossible to find an article or book that praises any one of these three plays as good literary art. The very nature of the plays as religious allegories has worked to their disadvantage, tempting critics to view them as dramatized rhetoric and to discount their artistry as craft in the service of religion. But such an attitude prejudges the plays, imposing generalized standards of what constitutes good art. No matter how comfortable it is to hold such standards—universal touchstones, if you will—they don't produce very accurate, informed critical evaluations.

To be sure, scholars have given their full share of objective attention to the three plays, studying their sources in sermons of the period, their genre, their language, their influences on later works, and even their performance and staging. But there is an important difference between literary scholarship and literary criticism—a distinction between knowledge and evaluation. We now *know* a great deal about these plays, and the time to evaluate them as art seems long overdue.

Although my own sense of how to evaluate literature as art will become clear in the following analyses of the three Macro plays, a few comments at this point might help to put the theory that underlies my analyses into perspective. In any historical period, the writer as artist is ultimately a maker; he selects literary and linguistic components and arranges them in some specific relationship to one another. The job of the critic is first to identify the various structural components in a particular work, then to determine what principle or organizing design—what form—relates the components to one another, and finally to judge whether that particular form causes those various structural components to cohere. If its form relates the components to one another consistently and harmoniously, the work is artistically successful. Because every art work is unique, the kinds of relationships and the kinds of formal coherence are almost unlimited, and no universal standard or standards are applicable. The coherence of structural components in a work depends on the nature and kind of components in that work and the fittingness of the particular form or principle of organization that relates them. For an artistic evaluation to be objectively valid (at least for it to be as objective as possible), we must abstract the standards for that evaluation from each particular work, not impose the standards from outside, based on taste, prejudice, or some generalized sense of the ideal qualities found in all good works of art. That's why we aren't being good critics when we say that all morality plays are bad art, and why we aren't dealing with the plays as art when we say they are dull, or dry, or learned, or stiff. Literary criticism only makes sense when it deals with a particular work as good or bad, and when it uses standards for evaluation based on the formal relationships that link the structures in that particular work. Of course, there are other things we value in literary works besides their artistry—often we value these other things more than the artistry—and we may well be able to apply universal standards of taste, morality, truth, and so forth to these nonartistic evaluations. The important thing is that we carefully distinguish among the various values so that we don't judge the artistry of a work by standards appropriate to some other legitimate quality.

I learned what I know about the process of criticism and the theory of literature that underlies it from Professor William Rooney at Catholic University and from the writings of the late James Craig LaDrière, who also was at Catholic University and then at Harvard. Professor Helmut Hatzfeld of Catholic University taught me to analyze style. Over the years, I've blended some of their ideas together, made some minor adjustments here and there, forgotten some of what I learned, and made up a few new things of my own. I owe my introduction to medieval literature and to *The Castle of Perseverance* to Professor E. Catherine Dunn, also of Catholic University, who hinted years ago that there may be more to that play than critics have generally supposed. O. B. Hardison, director of the Folger Shakespeare Library, has encouraged me over the many years I've been thinking about these plays, and the librarians and curators at the Folger Library, the Mullen Memorial Library at Catholic University, the National Gallery of Art in Washington, D.C., the Fenwick Library at George Mason University, and the British Museum have all been patient and helpful.

I owe an immense debt of gratitude to my mother, Mary Kelley, and to Lisa Henry and her family, who shared the burden of keeping my five-year-old son, Owen, happily busy so I could have the blocks of time necessary to write this book. Sheryn Johnson helped in the tedious process of locating books and articles, making the joy of scholarship even more delightful. George Mason University kindly awarded me a small grant to cover the costs of indexing the book, thus saving me from a pleasant but time-consuming task, and for that, and the efforts of Louanne Wheeler which it supported, I am indeed grateful.

I wish to thank the Council of the Early English Text Society for graciously granting me permission to quote extensively from their edition of *The Macro Plays*, edited by Mark Eccles.

Selections from three lyrics, "The Mother and Her Son on the Cross," "Mary Complains to Other Mothers," and "The Fear of Death Confounds Me," included in *Medieval English Lyrics*, edited by R. T. Davies, are reproduced here by kind permission of Northwestern University Press, who published the book in the United States, and by Faber and Faber, Ltd., London, the original publishers.

A part of chapter 2 originally appeared as "Fifteenth-Century Flamboyant Style and *The Castle of Perseverance*," in *Comparative Drama* 6 (1972): 14–27, copyright by the Editors of *Comparative Drama*, and I thank them for permission to reprint sections of it here.

With all this help and encouragement, I have no one to blame but myself for whatever might not make good sense in the pages that follow.

Michael R. Kelley

Fairfax, Virginia
November 1978

Chapter 1
Introduction

Beginning in the mid-fourteenth century and extending into the sixteenth, English writers experimented with a type of play we now call the morality. These dramatized allegories, apparently based on contemporary sermons and penitential literature, repeated familiar teachings about the nature of sin, the need for repentance, and the ever-present availability of God's mercy. Thus, at the same time that the medieval mystery cycles were dramatically presenting a panoramic history of the human race, from the creation to the last judgment, the moralities were dramatizing a similar story individualized to the life of a single human being typifying all mankind. The basic plot sequence of both the mysteries and the moralities is that of innocence/fall/redemption, and every morality, like every cycle, displays this underlying pattern.[1] Where the cycle plays put Christ, His passion, death, and resurrection at their dramatic center, the moralities place Mankind, as the recipient of Christ's mercy, at their center.

Though probably many more were written and performed,

only five medieval English moralities have survived the ravages of time, vandalism, and religious prejudice. Of these, *Pride of Life* (ca. 1346)[2] is the earliest and exists only as a fragment, though introductory "banns"—the medieval equivalent of our modern movie previews—provide an outline of the whole plot. The latest, *Everyman* (ca. 1500),[3] is undoubtedly the best known and most admired, quite possibly because it has been performed so frequently since its first modern staging in London on July 13, 1901.[4] In addition to being more popular than the other moralities, *Everyman* is the only one of the group to begin after its hero has already fallen from innocence into sin. Some lists of medieval moralities also include *Youth* (ca. 1513),[5] *Hickscorner* (ca. 1515),[6] and *Mundus et Infans* (ca. 1520).[7] Having chosen the year 1500 as the cutoff date for the Middle Ages in England, I would group these with the many other religious moralities written during the Renaissance.

The remaining three medieval moralities, the only ones from the fifteenth century, survived into modern times bound together in a single volume once owned (and apparently never shared with anyone) by an eighteenth-century Anglican antiquarian, Rev. Cox Macro (1683–1737, *D.N.B.*), under whose name, unhappily, the plays continue to be identified.[8] In this group is the longest and most schematically complete morality, *The Castle of Perseverance* (ca. 1425), the most theologically expository and least dramatic of the eight, *Wisdom* (ca. 1466), and the raunchiest, most scatological, and hence most maligned of the group, *Mankind* (ca. 1467). These three moralities from the last century of the English Middle Ages have much in common, yet each presents the basic sequence of innocence/fall/redemption in a completely different way. A study of the plays' similarities and differences can tell us a great deal about late medieval style, aesthetics, and theatricality.

The first modern reference to any of the Macro plays came

in 1823 when William Hone remarked on the stage plan of *The Castle of Perseverance*.[9] Two years later, Thomas Sharp printed a facsimile of that plan and mentioned that the manuscript was from Macro's collection then owned by Hudson Gurney.[10] But it was not until 1904 that the three plays were published together in a single volume.[11] *Mankind* received its first modern performance in New York in December, 1910.[12] *The Castle of Perseverance* was first produced in 1938.[13] To my knowledge, *Wisdom* has escaped modern performance altogether.

The plays have had numerous known owners besides Macro. At the end of *Wisdom* and at the end of *Mankind*, Latin inscriptions translate: "O book, if anyone shall perhaps ask to whom you belong, you will say, 'I belong above everything to Hyngham a monk.'" Mark Eccles (whose edition of the plays for the Early English Text Society supplants the 1904 edition) believes the handwriting of the inscription to be late fifteenth century, and notes that a monk of Bury St. Edmunds Abbey in Suffolk, named Thomas Hyngham wrote his name as owner in a fifteenth-century manuscript of Boethius.[14] Others whose names appear, either in normal script or in ciphers, include one Robert Oliver, a Thomas Wyllam, and Richard Cake of Bury, Senior. Since August 1936, the plays have been owned by the Folger Library in Washington, D.C.

There is still no definite consensus about where or by whom the plays were written. All three are clearly in the East Midlands dialect, and the handwriting of the manuscript (though not the hand of the authors of the plays) seems to point to Norfolk for the scribe who copied *The Castle of Perseverance* and Suffolk for the other scribe who copied both *Mankind* and *Wisdom*.[15] Linguistic and stylistic evidence indicates that each play had a separate author, but enough similarities exist to suggest that the authors may well have known each other, or at least may have known each other's work. The reference to Bury in line 274 of *Mankind*, the possibility that an early owner of *Wisdom* and *Mankind* may have been a monk of Bury, the chance that a large number of Macro's manuscripts had originally belonged to the abbey library at Bury (which in the fifteenth century was a large and powerful Benedictine monastery and home of the poet-monk John Lydgate) suggest that *Mankind* and *Wisdom*, at least, and perhaps even *The Castle of Perseverance*, were written or revised by monks at the abbey.[16]

Traditionally, the Benedictines were not a preaching order, but as the power and influence of the preaching orders of Dominicans, Franciscans, and Augustinians increased in the later Middle Ages—orders whose members mingled with the people, instructing them in faith and morals through sermons and devotional manuals—the Benedictines may have decided to use drama as one way for them to reach outside the monastery and to teach and inspire laymen. A traveling play would have been an ideal device for spreading Benedictine instruction, since it could present its message throughout the countryside while its author remained in his monastery, following the communal life of work and prayer that distinguishes the Benedictines from most other religious orders of the time. The high level of theological learning exhibited in each of these plays further supports a monastic provenance.[17]

The need to establish the origins and identify the authors of the Macro plays isn't nearly as urgent as the need to reassess them aesthetically. The plays have received a generally bad press, being denounced rather soundly both for their apparently wooden, allegorical characters and for their lengthy speeches of moral instruction.[18] At best, the moralities have been viewed as transitional aberrations between medieval and Renaissance drama, valuable primarily for what they can tell us about the evolutionary progression from the simple "Quem Queritis" trope to the glories of Shakespeare.[19] Seldom if at all have these plays been treated as works of true dramatic art or judged by standards appropriate to their literary nature. *Mankind*, for example, was condemned, as recently as twenty-three years ago, as a theologically ignorant play.[20] Whether or not that judgment is sound, it has little bearing on the play's dramatic value. Because *The Castle of Perseverance* is early, full in scope, and a virtual commonplace book of morality play elements, it has fared little better, receiving more than the usual amount of historical and developmental attention, at the consequent expense of artistic and theatrical evaluation. When literary judgments have been offered about the moralities they have usually been little more than sweeping generalizations. E. K. Chambers, for example, thought *Wisdom* was "clumsily written,"[21] and Hardin Craig called it "over-worded and . . . not dramatically effective."[22] More recently, Stanley Kahrl avoids a truly literary judgment of *Mankind* when he writes that the play "is particularly interesting in its use of vulgarity and slapstick comedy to achieve its desired effect . . . a good collection from the audience."[23]

The Macro plays, like the other English moralities, exhibit many of the stylistic traits that historians of fifteenth-century art and architecture have come to call "flamboyant," and it will be difficult, if not impossible, to appreciate the plays fully without first understanding the characteristics of this style, reflecting as it does the taste of its age and the consequent aesthetic expectations of contemporary audiences. Every epoch or period style is of course basically a generalization, since it is simply a cluster of stylistic traits that have been abstracted from representative works of a period and considered, for classification purposes, as an objective entity. Even though grounded in particular examples drawn from contemporary works, the concept of a period style can never be rigorously precise or totally representative. Its primary value is that it reveals basic trends in taste and provides a cultural overview of

1. Rose window at Chartres Cathedral (ca. 1150). Photograph courtesy Roger Viollet, Paris

2. Rose Window, south transept at Sens Cathedral (ca. 1490).
Photograph courtesy Roger Viollet, Paris

the specific period under discussion. Such an overview can nevertheless be helpful in that it can serve as a grid for determining the extent to which any individual work from a given age is representative of its time, and it can explain, in terms of the tastes of that time, the existence of features which may seem strange or even unpleasant to more modern tastes.

Historians of Continental art, literature, and architecture who have identified flamboyant style find that it was originally a product of the Franco-Burgundian culture, which flourished from the late fourteenth through the fifteenth century in the geographic region including Flanders, the duchies of Burgundy and Berry, and most of northern France.[24] Since England was closely allied both politically and economically with the Burgundian court during this time, it's not surprising that many characteristics of Continental flamboyant style should be found in English art and literature.

We first find the term "flamboyant" used to describe central and northern French cathedral architecture of the late fourteenth and fifteenth century which decorated facades with complex and elaborately ornate flamelike curves and countercurves instead of the pointed arches and rounded curves used during the high Gothic period.[25] The rose windows of the cathedrals at Chartres (ca. 1150) and Sens (ca. 1490), shown in Figures *1* and *2*, are striking examples of the two styles and the contrast between them. English cathedrals constructed at the end of the Middle Ages also display a heightened embellishment and elaboration of the stone tracery, but in England, where the style is called perpendicular Gothic, the curvilinearity that marks the French style at Sens and elsewhere is not a central feature of the decoration. Once past the elaborate flamboyant facades and inside the fifteenth-century cathedrals, we find a more functional use of space; the forests of pillars are gone, and these flamboyant cathedrals seem more open and practical in their use of interior space.[26] This blending of elaboration with functionalism in the cathedrals of the period has parallels in both the visual arts and the literature of the fifteenth century, and "flamboyant" is a particularly appropriate term for the style of these arts as well, since like the effect in architecture, sumptuous ornamentation is its most readily distinguishable feature.

In visual art, the period's love for complex decoration resulted in the ornamental use of symbolism and the decorative personification of abstract thoughts. Nearly every idea was given a figurative shape, a personal form.[27] This delight in thinking symbolically and allegorically was accompanied by a desire to depict every minute detail, a tendency which fostered a scrupulous concern for realistic, perceptual accuracy.[28] These two opposing stylistic concerns fuse in the art of the period to produce the intermixture of abstraction or symbolism and concretion or "realism," both elaborated to extremes, which is the most distinctive characteristic of Flemish painting.

In Van Eyck's *The Annunciation* (Figure 3), painted in the first quarter of the fifteenth century, minute, realistic details abound. The robe and wings of the Angel; the distinction of textures, from the hard polished floor to the covering on the footstool and the tiny pearl cluster which forms the end of the Virgin's bookmark; the natural use of light and shadow, the detailed depiction of scenes from the Old Testament, and animal signs of the zodiac on the floor, all contribute to the painting's ornate visual realism. At the same time, the entire painting is charged with symbolic meaning. Samson and David, pictured on the floor tiles, and Isaac and Jacob, whose pictures decorate the apse wall, are each symbolic prefigurations of Christ; the Dove and beams of light emanating from it symbolize the Third Person of the Trinity, bringing the light of Grace; the upper story of the room, in relative darkness, is illuminated by a single window symbolic of the Old Testament order, while the Virgin kneels in the light cast by a triple window symboliz-

3. *The Annunciation* by Jan van Eyck. Courtesy of the National Gallery of Art, Washington. Andrew W. Mellon Collection

ing the New Testament order, the revelation of which begins with the event the painting celebrates.[29] Huizinga sees this kind of duality—symbolism and detailed realism together—as resulting from the "aesthetic sentiment" of an age which delighted in both "the dignity and sanctity of the subject," and "the astonishing mastery, the perfectly natural rendering of all details."[30] By blending symbolism and realism, the stylistic response to this dual delight produces a higher degree of ornateness than could be achieved through either style alone.

A duality of stylistic features analogous to that found in fifteenth-century architecture and painting was used in the composition of literary works. Allegory, symbolism, personification, and the other figures and tropes usually associated with the high style of rhetorical figuration, exist alongside elements which add earthly, perceptual realism: little anecdotal details, highly focused visual descriptions, lengthy catalogues of specific places or things, particularized homely similes, scenes from simple, everyday life, and bits of sexual or excremental vulgarity. Authors frequently switch from one style to the other in a completely natural and unselfconscious way.[31] As in the other arts of the period, this flamboyant mixture creates a heightened degree of decoration, since the realistic details join with the devices of rhetorical figuration to add a contrasting decoration, a kind of ornamental particularity.

We can see this duality clearly in a work like *Jacob's Well*, an early fifteenth-century devotional treatise on the seven deadly sins.[32] In this extended allegory, Confession—with six qualifying attributes—is presented as a shovel, with a six-part handle, used to dig out the hard ooze of deadly sin from the bottom of the well. Intermixed with this elaborate allegory, we find a number of particular examples which create vividly realistic pictures to further ornament the passage and reinforce the more general message of the allegory. For example, the fifth part of the handle of confession is frequent confession, and in the midst of this allegorically based image, the author inserts a vivid example, unrelated to the figure of the shovel. He reminds the reader that if a shirt is worn all year long without being washed it will be "right foul," and a launderer will not be able to get it as clean and white as if it were washed once a week throughout the year. The author then applies this example to frequent confession which will cleanse the soul more effectively than occasional confession. The example of the shirt stands out in the passage because of its homeliness and realistic practicality, and because it departs so completely from the image of the shovel which is being used as the perceptual basis of the allegorical construct in this section. The abruptness of the transition back to the original allegory, with its unavoidable blend of images, underscores the stylistic mixture even more. "Therefore, be often washed in your confession and then you shall be clean, for the more often your shovel shall cast out the ooze, the sooner will your pit be clean."[33] The allegory at this point has a perceptual side, identifying confession with the shovel, and the example of the shirt adds another layer of perceptual realism to the passage, giving additional concreteness to the meaning and creating in the process a higher degree of elaboration.

The desire to concretize every abstract thought, to decorate each concept or idea with layers of perceptual, often homely, examples, resulted in the mixing of allegory with concrete exemplification, which is one of the most characteristic features of literary flamboyant style. In order to achieve this effect, fifteenth-century writers borrowed and then exaggerated features from two previously existing medieval literary styles. One of these, the ornate, highly conventional style, had been used since the twelfth century to create works which required an elevated level of stylistic ornamentation. Charles Muscatine calls this the "conventional style of the courtly tradition," a style that makes extensive use of rhetorical colors and figures, including allegory, symbolism, elevated diction, repetition, and balance.[34] Its visual images are usually idealized, and there is less concern with detailed accuracy than with recognizable conventions. The other style, which Muscatine calls the "realistic style of the bourgeois tradition," also can be traced back to the twelfth century.[35] It is naturalistic and even vulgar at times in its descriptions of reality and relatively free of rhetorical ornaments.[36] Instead, there is a literalness and a concern with homely details which make this medieval realism seem almost modern.

Each style is found alone (in the courtly lyric and romance, on the one hand, and the beast fables and fabliaux, on the other);[37] the two merge earlier than the fifteenth century in Jean de Meun's thirteenth-century continuation of *Le Roman de la Rose* and are found together in almost every one of Chaucer's *Canterbury Tales*.[38] Erich Auerbach saw evidence of this same mixture as early as the patristic period and viewed it as a fundamental feature of Christian literature, based ultimately on the sublimity and humility of Christ's passion.[39] The essential difference between this earlier blend of the two contrasting styles and their mixture in the late fourteenth and fifteenth centuries is not so much one of kind as of degree. The flamboyant blend of realism and rhetorical figuration is a duality of extremes where the essential characteristics of each of the two traditional styles are exaggerated for an increased ornamental effect. Highly perceptual details further embellish the concrete images used in the creation of extended, elaborate allegories, and this mixture of detailed examples, lengthy, specific catalogues, and vivid descriptions with the ornate rhetorical figures and colors of the courtly style creates a much higher level of ornamentation and embellishment than anything that had gone before.[40] Detail functions as decoration (as it does in

Van Eyck's depiction of the Angel's wings), and the dual delight of the fifteenth century in ornateness and in giving a concrete shape to every concept is fully satisfied.

The realistic style is exaggerated in the secular and religious art and literature of the period, but is especially evident in those works dealing with the sufferings of Christ. Here we find an increased emphasis on the intimate and personal details and a measurably heightened emotionality of tone.[41] Mathis Grünewald's *Small Crucifixion* (ca. 1475) is a good example of this stylistic concern with the details of suffering in fifteenth-century painting (see Figure 4), and the following stanza from a lyric of the period illustrates the same concern in literature.

Behold! wemen, when that ye play,
And have youre childer on kne   [*dancing on your knee*]
   daunsand,
Ye fele ther fete, so fete ar thay,   [*fat*]
And to your sight full well likand.   [*thoroughly enjoyable*]
But the most finger of mine hand   [*largest*]
Throrow my sonis fete I may put here,   [*through*]
And pulle it out sore bledand   [*sorely bleeding*]
For now lyeth dedd my dere son, dere.[42]

Compare this to a late thirteenth-century lyric on the same subject, with its much more subdued realism.

"Stond well, moder, under Rode.   [*cross*]
Behold thy sone with glade mode—   [*happy heart*]
Blithe moder might thou be."   [*cheerful*]
"Sone, how shulde I blithe stonde?
I se thine fet, I se thine honde,   [*feet*]
Nailed to the harde tre."[43]

In addition to the exaggeration of detailed realism, we find the other stylistic side of the flamboyant duality pushed to an

4. *The Small Crucifixion* by Mathis Grünewald. Courtesy of the
National Gallery of Art, Washington. Samuel H. Kress Collection

ornamental extreme. Poets elaborated and extended their allegories far beyond any possible functional use to the point where their creation was, as Huizinga notes, an intellectual pastime, a kind of literary game.[44] An example of this sheer delight in the creation of allegories—and such examples are easy to find in the fifteenth century—is the English work *Jacob's Well*, mentioned earlier. This ornate and extended allegory depicts man's body as a well fed by five streams—the five senses—each of which can admit the deadly waters of sin to the well. The soul lies in this pit of foul water and cries out to be saved from drowning in the cursed waters of sin. The bottom of the well is covered with the ooze of the seven deadly sins, and this ooze must be cleaned out with the shovel of confession, down to the solid ground of the seven virtues, so the soul won't be trapped in the mire. At this lower level are seven clear springs: the seven gifts of the Holy Ghost, and as they fill the well with clear water, the five water gates of the senses must be shut tightly to prevent the curse of sin from reentering the well. Once cleansed, the well can be shored up with the stones of faith; Christ can come to refresh Himself with the waters of grace, and at death, the soul can climb out of the well to heaven on the ladder of charity. This drawn-out allegory, and others like it, clearly must have been produced at least partly for the sheer joy of it, as display pieces, presenting well-known doctrines in delightfully different and ornate ways.[45]

Allegory was by no means the only device popular with writers of the period. Figures, tropes, and other schemes of meaning, as well as figures of sound—elaborate verse and rhyme patterns, alliterative groupings, and multisyllabic aureate terms borrowed from French and Latin all added further embellishment. We learn from occasional passages of literary appreciation that the ability to embellish and ornament the language of a work with rhetorical colors was highly prized, even considered to be one of the essential qualities of a good poet. The great esteem accorded Chaucer in the fifteenth century was almost wholly based on his facility in embellishing the language. Caxton writes, for example, "Therefore the worshipful fader & first foundeur & enbelissher of ornate eloquence in our englissh I mene Maister Geffrey Chaucer hath translated this said werke out of latyn in to oure vsual and moder tonge."[46]

The essence of literary flamboyant style, then, is its ornamental mixture of detailed realistic description with those rhetorical devices associated with the high style of courtly idealism, including allegory, symbol, and the other decorative figures of sound and meaning, to achieve a higher level of ornamentation than would be possible with either style alone. The realistic elements in flamboyant style do not produce the same effects as modern realism (though the term "realism" is useful here as long as we keep the distinction clear), nor is flamboyant style ornate in the same way that the earlier medieval style of courtly idealism was ornate. Rather, by combining, and more particularly, exaggerating the devices of bourgeois realism and courtly idealism, flamboyance achieves a peculiar two-leveled embellishment perfectly suited to the dual fifteenth-century delights in ornamentation and detailed particularization.

What created the delight in such exaggerated ornamentation and encouraged this mixture of styles during the fifteenth century is far more difficult to determine than it is to recognize that such a taste did indeed exist at the time. Throughout the Middle Ages, the court and aristocracy had provided the necessary patronage for artists and writers. As the feudal system began to break down, beginning perhaps with the first visitation of the Black Plague (ca. 1348) and the subsequent rise of urban centers, a new bourgeois middle class arose, and many of its members were wealthy enough to become patrons of the arts themselves.[47] These rich bourgeoisie enjoyed detailed, homely realism, yet they also sought the luxury and ostentation once available only to the aristocracy. At the same time, the aristocracy, which continued to patronize the arts (though by now no longer exclusively), got the chance to enjoy the increased realism in some of the works being produced for bourgeois patrons, and this was for them and for the artists they sponsored a delightful novelty. We see this in the works of Chaucer, who made extensive, though not exaggerated, use of bourgeois elements in pieces he wrote for the court. It would be an oversimplification to say that each of the two classes merely developed a taste for the other's style of art. But clearly, some cross-pollination did occur and resulted in the blending of the two styles, each in somewhat exaggerated form, perhaps because of the bourgeoisie's desire to outplay the aristocracy at their own game and the aristocracy's response, going the bourgeoisie one better.

Flamboyance may also be seen as a medieval mannerism, whose magnified features can be traced to the inevitable social and artistic forces that accompany the close of every long-lasting historical period.[48] Respect for, and the desire to emulate earlier masters—and at the same time contribute something of their own making—encouraged artists and writers of the fifteenth century to borrow techniques they admired in earlier works and embellish them. Art turned back upon art, and ornamentation became an end in itself.

In addition to understanding the style in which fifteenth-century artists expressed themselves, we will benefit from a knowledge of the favored commonplaces of the period and the information such knowledge can provide about the artistic temperament and taste of the time. Perhaps in response to the many visitations of the great plague from the mid-fourteenth century onward, and the continued devastation of the Hundred Years' War, the theme of death and human decay became one of the major topics of the age. Huizinga notes that "no other epoch has laid so much stress as the expiring Middle Ages on

5. Illustration from *Disputacion Betwyx the Body and Wormes* (ca. 1438), British Museum Additional MS 37049, folio 32, verso. Reproduced by permission of the British Library

the thought of death," and the image was not consoling but frighteningly macabre.[49] Of course, a concern with death and the afterlife had long been a characteristic of Christian thought, but it was not until the fifteenth century that it reached such a gruesome intensity. For example, the skeleton is not found as a symbol of death until this period, when it suddenly appears everywhere in woodcuts, murals, and literary works celebrating the Dance of Death.[50] The bones are visible, as are shreds of rotting flesh, worms, frogs, and flies, in this recurring artistic motif where Death summons a variety of living victims. Clearly the dance is stylistically flamboyant in its fusing of allegory with grisly realism. This grim fascination with the effects of biological decay on the human body and the desire to use the image to reinforce moral instruction also resulted in the production of elaborately carved, macabre tombs and gravestones. Here, artists would depict the grotesquely rigid corpse, with worms crawling out of the ears, eyes, and bowels. Often this grossly realistic image would be accompanied by the serene figure of the corpse, lying in repose. A drawing of such a tomb in the English *Disputacion Betwyx the Body and Wormes* (ca. 1438) strikingly illustrates this stylistically flamboyant fifteenth-century practice (see Figure 5).[51]

Decay and Death were equally commonplace themes in sermons, lyrics, and dramas of the period, and the preoccupation gave rise to a genre of conduct literature on the art of dying— the *ars moriendi*.[52] Death functions didactically in all these works, serving to remind man of the transitoriness and vanity of this life and extolling the social doctrine (again perhaps in response to the rise of the bourgeoisie) that all men are equal in the face of death, the great leveller.[53] This social concept is poignantly expressed in a single stanza by the fifteenth-century poet, William Dunbar, though it has parallels in poems by late fourteenth-century writers like Gower, as well.

On to the ded gois all estatis,	[*On to death go all estates,*]
Princis, prelotis, and potestatis	[*prelates and potentates*]
Baith riche and pur of all degre.	[*Both rich and poor*]
Timor mortis conturbat me.[54]	[*The fear of death confounds me.*]

The fifteenth century continued to witness the outpouring of works of systematized religious instruction in response to the Church's repeated calls for the moral education of the laity.[55] These works covered the whole range of Christian doctrine necessary for salvation, but their special emphasis was on man's sins and his need for repentance through the sacrament of penance.[56] In fact, the number of English penitential works in the fourteenth and fifteenth centuries emphasizing the vices and virtues, usually in allegorical form, is so vast that the seven deadly sins and the seven cardinal virtues can be considered commonplaces of the period.[57] One of these treatises, Lorens d'Orléans's *Somme des Vices et des Vertues*, which paralleled Dan Michel's *Ayenbite of Inwyt*, and Caxton's *Royal Book*, existed in nine separate English versions between 1340 and 1486.[58]

Of the seven deadly sins—anger, avarice, envy, gluttony, lechery, pride, and sloth—avarice received special attention in the fifteenth century, becoming a commonplace in its own right. Again perhaps because of the rise of the merchant bourgeoisie, the sin of avarice became one of the most noticeable vices of both religious and secular society, and both Dominican and Franciscan preachers directed many of their sermons against it.[59] Though touching every social class and age group, avarice was considered to be the special sin of old age—a point of particular interest when we come to *The Castle of Perseverance*.

Possibly as a balance to the contemporary sermon's emphasis on man's sinful nature and as a way of preventing the laity from despairing completely in the face of their human weakness and predilection for sin, the idea of God's boundless mercy was especially emphasized in fifteenth-century writings. Mercy first appears allegorically in English at the beginning of the thirteenth century as one of the Four Daughters of God. This Four Daughters motif was developed around mid century into the feudal allegory, *Chasteau d'Amour* by Bishop Grosseteste. It occurs again in the *Cursor Mundi*, the *Gesta Romanorum*, the *Charter of the Abbey of the Holy Ghost*, and *Piers Plowman* during the fourteenth century. In the fifteenth century, versions of the allegory multiplied further, and at about this time Mercy came to have an allegorical existence apart from the other three.[60] Thus *The Castle of Perseverance* dramatizes the debate of all Four Daughters but gives Mercy more stanzas than the other three; *Mankind* features Mercy alone as a dominant (male) character throughout the play, and *Wisdom* emphasizes that without God's mercy salvation would be nearly impossible. When the morality play is viewed in terms of fifteenth-century commonplaces and stylistic practices, its contemporary appeal is easy to understand. Though no one of the three Macro plays displays every one of the major commonplaces of its time, what each does include was clearly familiar to its audience.

But it's in their style that the moralities make their greatest appeal to the fifteenth-century playgoer. The taste of the time for exaggerated ornamentation achieved through the mixture of realism and allegory would have surely been satisfied by an art form which uses live actors on a stage to present abstract concepts and qualities. By this device alone, the morality play achieves both a heightened degree of ornamentation and a perfect fusion of the two modes of stylistic expression.

Yet it is this very fusion of allegory and realism that creates serious dramatic difficulties for the morality playwright. Each character in a morality play functions on two levels at once:

the level of the abstraction which he presents, and the level of theatrical reality—the stage where the presentation occurs. With the exception of the hero—Mankind, Anima, Everyman, Youth—and perhaps God and the Devil as well, there is no natural or mimetic relationship between the actor or actress onstage and the abstract concept which he or she represents. In other words, the actors in a morality play don't actually *impersonate* Wisdom, or Charity, or Mankind, or Mercy. Instead, the actors simply present these abstract concepts.[61] Because of this distinction, it probably stretches the point somewhat to call the moralities drama, if by drama we mean that literary form involving impersonation, as well as action and dialogue.[62] Rather, the moralities are instructional demonstrations (celebrations, if you will) of Christian doctrine, not plays in the traditional sense.[63]

It is because of their demonstrational function that the characters seem one-dimensional. The vices must be consistently vicious, the virtues consistently virtuous. Charity can have no weak avaricious moments, and Mischief can never suffer a pang of conscience. All the characters must be totally consistent and unchanging (except Mankind, who must be consistently changeable), or the whole analogy will collapse like a house of cards.

This quality of their characters is a major reason why the moralities contain so much expository material. When Mankind falls into sin he can only do it symbolically, by verbally betrothing himself to Lechery, or swearing fidelity to New-guise, Nowadays, Nought, and so forth. Since the tempers and the sins are already present as characters in the play, they can't very well be present as actions too. The same is true of the virtues. When Mankind is in a state of grace, he demonstrates this by keeping company with the Virtues, by speaking in an identical stanza form with them, or by some other presentational device involving talk rather than action. In the play

Mankind, we do see Mankind working and praying, but that's because work and prayer are not characters in the play. If they were, we could only see Mankind talking with them. In a morality play, when Mankind goes to Confession he literally *goes to* Confession who embraces him and welcomes him to the state of grace.

Earlier critics were right in questioning characterization in the moralities, but we can see now that they questioned it from the wrong angle. The characters are not dry and lifeless because they are abstractions. In fact, they are not abstractions but actors presenting abstractions, and as actors they have life, voices, movement, and full theatrical vitality. It's more to the point to realize that the moralities are not true drama because of their characters, for no matter how lifelike the characters appear to be on the stage, they remain demonstrations rather than impersonations of psychological, doctrinal, and moral reality. In short, they are rooted in exposition, not imitation.

Most of the moralities have some elements of plot, usually involving physical human actions, and these tend to obscure the presentational nature of the characters and make them seem more dramatically conventional than they really are. Because they too are allegories, the plots, like the characters, can be understood on both a doctrinal level and a theatrical level. But unlike the characters who must often explain themselves to the audience in elaborate expository speeches outlining the concept they are presenting, there is usually enough dramatic motivation on the theatrical level to make the events in the plots understandable. We get the theatrical point that there are good and evil forces battling for a prize (Mankind) in *The Castle of Perseverance*, or that the hero of *Everyman* is deserted at his hour of greatest need by those he thought were his true friends. But we fall into a trap if we think of these characters as "friends" or "heroes" and "villains" or if we think they are really "fighting" or "deserting" in a truly mimetic sense.

Rather, the characters are often only aspects of a single human personality or facets of a complex set of moral beliefs, and the things they do are merely illustrations of some moral idea, since both actors and actions function as one side of a two-sided figure of speech designed to make the abstract concrete and visible.

Despite their unconventional characters and plots, the plays are theatrically successful because their dramatic format encourages us to pretend that the actors, with their human personalities, are actually impersonating real human beings rather than simply projecting abstract concepts, and that they are performing fictively believable human actions. The moralities are very much a literary anomaly and it's probably more accurate to think of them as dramatizations than as dramas, celebrating man's ultimate triumph over sin in a plotted form with dialogue and characters, which in their flamboyant complexity provide a spectacular feast for eye and ear that is entertaining theatre in the highest sense, but not Aristotelian drama.

Though the moral concepts they dramatize first appear in sermons of the period, it's important to recognize that most moralities are not, as some critics have maintained, simply dramatized sermons.[64] The plays do give moral information—demonstrating the pitfalls of sin and man's need to repent—but this is commonplace, familiar material by the time the moralities appear, and they present it so grandly and with such flamboyant ornamentation that their elaborate forms often eclipse the instruction. The plays do express some of the same ideas as the medieval sermons, but their form and their function are entirely different. The moralities are dramatizations using character and dialogue, sermons are monologue expositions; it's a contradiction in terms (at least it certainly is a blurring of distinctions) to think of the plays as dramatizations of sermons. In their function, as well, the plays differ from the sermons. The moralities never berate or chastise Mankind or their

25

audience for human failure. Instead, they treat moral weakness as a given feature of the human condition and remind their audience that man can achieve salvation in spite of his spiritually frail condition.

Though they may seem to use the specter of death as a device to frighten playgoers into getting their spiritual houses in order, each of the plays shows Mankind achieving salvation or spiritual reconciliation despite the fact that he has not been farsighted and prudent. In *The Castle of Perseverance*, the only one of the Macro plays where the hero dies, Mankind actually dies in mortal sin, crying out for mercy, and is saved from beyond the grave. In *Everyman*, another play where the death of the hero is dramatized, Death comes when Everyman is at the lowest point in his spiritual fortunes but gives him time to get his account book ready. In all the moralities we see Mankind yielding to temptation or in a state of sin, but the audience is so led to identify with the hero that there's no sense of "there but for the grace of God go I," but rather, the sense that "we're in this together; God's mercy is available to us all." Each of the plays begins as a potential tragedy and ends happily—not primarily because Mankind has learned his lesson in time, but because God's plan for Mankind's salvation is as strong as Mankind is weak. The emphasis on mercy is so pervasive in the plays that damnation seems almost an impossibility. To avoid that possible misunderstanding, the author of *Mankind* has Mercy say : "Synne not in hope of mercy; þat [that] is a cryme notary" (845). But despite the warning in this play, the moralities all seem to insist that eternal damnation is an exceedingly rare occurrence.

Rather than being polemical orations against sin, or even dramatized battles between vices and virtues, the moralities are dramatic reminders, showing where human weakness exists, pointing out appropriate responses to that weakness, and restating the need for contrition, sorrow, and the sacrament of confession. But more than anything else, the moralities are entertaining celebrations of the power of God's limitless mercy, reminding their audiences that His mercy is the ultimate source of salvation. By presenting these well-known truths in ornately embellished theatrical forms, the moralities delight more than they preach or teach, and their audiences today (like those in the fifteenth century) are more likely to feel entertained than preached at.

In their own time, the message of the moralities was one of hope. When death was striking with unexpected fury during the plagues, when greed and perjury, class upheaval, political instability, and war were bringing the established order into chaos, when Lollards and Nominalists were questioning the authority of the Church and man's ability to know the truth, the moralities must have been a welcome celebration of the medieval Christian's belief that God was still in His heaven, and that mankind could triumph over death through eternal salvation.

Much has been written about the Macro plays from historical, theological, linguistic, allegorical, and even theatrical points of view. Far less has been said about the plays as dramatic structures in the context of the style and art of their time. In the next three chapters we will look at *The Castle of Perseverance*, *Mankind*, and *Wisdom* in turn, viewing each in terms of style, theatricality, and structure so that we today may better understand and enjoy the plays as their original audience must have done.

Though written at different times by different authors, the three plays share a surprising number of elements in common. Each presents a progressive sequence of man-in-grace/ man-in-sin/ man-restored-to-grace. Each urges that man continue to fight against sin. Each emphasizes mankind's dependence on God's mercy for salvation. Each presents dramatic spectacle through music, song, and mime. Each involves elaborate costuming and staging more reminiscent of grand opera than of straight drama. Each details the World, Flesh, and Devil as the three enemies of man. Each emphasizes the theme of penitence, and provides for its hero to confess his sins. And finally, through the heterogeneous combination of perceptual realism and rhetorical figuration, homely detail and elaborate allegory, plotted sequences and informative expositions, each clearly manifests the whole panoply of stylistic and structural features which allows it to be classified as medieval flamboyant drama.

Chapter 2
Circles within Circles
The Castle of Perseverance

Since *The Castle of Perseverance* is the longest, the oldest, and the most complex—structurally and theologically—of the three Macro plays, it seems appropriate for us to defer to its age and size and begin our discussion with this formidable commonplace book of fifteenth-century dramatic allegory.

The play presents a balanced series of moral reversals in the long life of Mankind, beginning at a point shortly after his baptism as a young man and ending after his death as an old man when Mercy intercedes to save him from hell. Mankind is first persuaded to a life of sin by Bad Angel and introduced to World, Flesh, and Devil with their attendant cohorts, the seven deadly sins. After some time in sin, Mankind is rescued from this evil life by Confession and Penance and taken to the castle of perseverance to be protected by seven virtues or moral shields against the sins: Abstinence, Charity, Chastity, Generosity, Humility, Industry, and Patience. The castle is then besieged by the seven sins, six of whom are repulsed by their virtuous opposites. But Mankind has grown old, and the sin of age, Sir Covetous, successfully coaxes him out of the castle and back into a life of mortal sin. Then Death comes; Mankind dies in sin with a cry for Mercy on his lips, and his soul is carried off to hell by Bad Angel. The play ends with a debate in heaven among the Four Daughters of God: Mercy, Peace, Justice, and Truth. Mercy and Peace win the debate and Mankind is rescued from hell to dwell in eternal bliss. Other characters figuring in the action are God, a Good Angel (Bad Angel's virtuous counterpart), Backbiter (World's messenger), Lust-liking and Folly (two of World's companions), the Soul of Mankind, and an unnamed stranger simply called "boy" who is heir to the wealth that Mankind can't take with him to the grave. The play includes an impressive total of thirty-three separate roles, requiring a cast of at least twenty-two if allowance is made for role-doubling.[1]

Twelve stanzas announcing information about the performance are included in the manuscript and suggest that *The Castle of Perseverance* was performed as a touring play.[2] The text indicates that two flag-bearers or heralds proclaimed these stanzas or "banns" to the citizens of a town one week before a scheduled performance of the play, supplying the name of the appropriate town or village as they traveled around the countryside. In order to whet the local citizens' appetite and encourage their attendance at the upcoming performance, the banns summarize the plot and provide a little information about what the performance will be like. The heralds say that roles will be played in costumes of royal array and they mention that props will be used (132, 134). The play will be performed outside "on þe grene" (134) during daylight hours, and although neither the banns nor the text of the play mentions an admission charge, there is nothing to indicate that the performance was free.

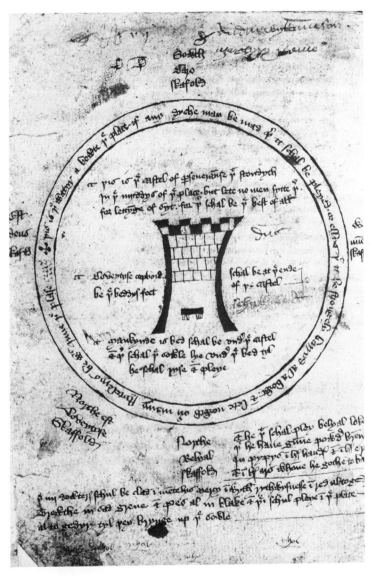

6. Stage plan of *The Castle of Perseverance* in the Macro Manuscript. By permission of the Folger Shakespeare Library

The stage plan included in the manuscript (see Figure 6), recommending as it does that the playing area be surrounded by a water-filled ditch or else be "strongly barryd [barred] al abowt" (possibly to keep out nonpaying spectators), also suggests that there may have been an admission charge for the play. The plan—the earliest known to exist in English drama —shows that the play was performed in the round and supplies detailed information about the placement of scaffolds or raised stages for the principal characters, the location of the castle structure in the center of the circle—with a bed and chest under it—the color of costumes for the Four Daughters of God, and the battle array for Belyal, the Devil.

The Castle of Perseverance is stylistically flamboyant, blending decorative rhetorical figuration with vivid bourgeois realism to produce an ornate stylistic duality that affects each major structural component. We notice the flamboyance immediately since the play's characters, though allegorically presenting abstract concepts, introduce themselves to us in ways that appeal to our senses and make them seem vividly concrete. World opens the play and embellishes his speech with the detailed specifics of a travelogue by enumerating a total of twenty-four countries, cities, and provinces that are under his dominion, "Assarye, Acaye, and Almayne,/ Cauadoyse, Capadoyse, and Cananee,/ Babyloyne, Brabon, Burgoyne, and Bretayne" (170–72), and so on.

The Devil, whose reality needed little stylistic reinforcement to be imagined by a medieval English playgoer, uses specific visual images from daily life for grimly comic as well as decorative purposes in his initial speech of self-description.

Now I sytte, Satanas, in my sad synne,	[*dark sin*]
As deuyl dowty, in draf as a drake.	[*valiant; in filth as a dragon*]
I champe and I chafe, I chocke on my chynne,	[*chomp; fume; thrust out my chin*]

I am boystows and bold, as Belyal þe blake.	[*fierce and bold*]
What folk þat I grope þei gapyn and grenne,	[*that I grab; gape and grimace*]
I wys fro Carlylle into Kent my carpynge þei take,	[*I know, my rebuke*]
Bothe þe bak and þe buttoke brestyth al on brenne,	[*burst forth in flames*]
Wyth werkys of wreche I werke hem mykyl wrake.	[*vengeance; cause them much pain*]

(196–203)[3]

In his opening speech, Flesh describes himself as being adorned with flowers and surrounded by taffeta tapestries, concrete items of visual splendor that symbolize the self-pampering which sins of the flesh entail. He was undoubtedly portrayed by a big-bellied actor, or one made to look that way, for he begins his self description with reference to his great paunch.

I byde as a brod brustun-gutte abouyn on þese tourys.	[*big bursting gut; above*]
Euerybody is þe betyr þat to myn byddynge is bent.	
I am Mankyndys fayre Flesch, florchyd in flowrys.	[*adorned*]

(235–37)

Mankind's opening speech is especially interesting as the first of many instances in the play where a peculiar kind of emotionally charged and homely realism, arising out of the fifteenth-century preoccupation with the miseries of human life, is used by an abstract figure.[4] Mankind's appearance in the nude provides strong additional reinforcement of his physical reality.

33

Aftyr oure forme-faderys kende
Þis nyth I was of my modyr born.   [*This night*]
Fro my modyr I walke, I wende,
Ful feynt and febyl I fare ȝou beforn.   [*I come before you*]
I am nakyd of lym and lende   [*limb and loin*]
As Mankynde is schapyn and schorn.
I not wedyr to gon ne to lende   [*to go or stay*]
To helpe myself mydday nyn morn.
   For schame I stonde and schende.   [*stand and am confused*]
I was born þis nyth in blody ble   [*condition*]
And nakyd I am, as ȝe may se.   [*you may see*]
A, Lord God in trinite,
   Whow Mankende is vnthende!   [*How feeble is Mankind*]

.   .   .   .

Coryows Criste, to ȝou I calle   [*loving; to you I call*]
As a grysly gost I grucche and grone,   [*frightful; I moan and groan*]
   I wene, ryth ful of thowth   [*fear*]
A, Lord Jhesu, wedyr may I goo?   [*go*]
A crysme I haue and no moo.   [*baptism cloth; no more*]
Alas, man may be wondyr woo   [*amazingly woeful*]
   Whanne þei be fyrst forth browth.   [*brought forth*]
                                      (275–87, 320–26)

The impact of Mankind's expression of emotional helplessness is heightened by its contrast with the shrill, boastful, and pompous speeches of World, Devil, and Flesh which have immediately preceded it.

Throughout the play, Mankind is designated as *Humanum Genus* and he typifies the entire human race, referring in his opening speech and elsewhere in the play to the general human condition he symbolically presents. Yet, he consistently uses the singular personal pronoun when referring to himself, and he functions within the plot as a single, particularized individual, not as a generalized representative of the race. The result of this shift of reference and dramatic function is a flamboyant fusion of the abstract and the concrete, the general and the particular.

The stage plan's specific details about costuming show the producers' concern with concrete realism in the portrayal of abstract characters. One note provides a graphic picture of the Devil's battle accoutrements: "he þat [that] schal pley belyal loke [be sure] þat he haue gunnepowdyr brennynge [burning] In pypys [pipes] in hys handys and in hys erys [ears] and in hys ars [ass] whanne he gothe to batayl." This is stark earthly realism indeed for a spiritual character, prompting some wonder about whether the same actor could play Belyal in more than one performance. His flaming orifices would certainly make the Devil a memorable dramatic character.

The other note of interest in the plan concerns the costumes of the Four Daughters of God, again illustrating the fifteenth-century delight in combining realism with symbolic ornamentation. Although these four characters represent abstract qualities in the mind of God, great stress was obviously placed on their concrete presentation and the color symbolism involved in it: "þe iiij [four] dowterys schul be clad in mentelys [mantles], Mercy in wyth [white], rythwysnesse [justice] in red altogedyr, Trewthe in sad [dark] grene, and Pes al in blake, and þei schul pleye in þe place altogedyr tyl þey [they] brynge up þe sowle."

It may be easier for us to outline the extent of the play's stylistic duality if we look at each style separately and note how its features are exaggerated. Much of the particularized realism in this (and all the moralities) comes from the use of live actors to portray the allegorical abstractions on the stage—a source of realism we miss when reading the plays. One-dimensional characters like Sloth, Industry, or Charity, who seem abstract and are difficult to imagine when presented as lines of dialogue, come alive when we see them walking around on the grass, talking with one another, and engaging in various kinds of theatrical horseplay. Each actor injects his own personality into the character he plays, or at very least his own cartoonish notion of the abstraction, and by this infusion the character becomes that much more vivid.

The performance included songs, trumpet fanfares, colorful banners, elaborate costumes, and a great many hand props—in short, the whole panoply of realistic assaults on the senses that a full-scale, no-holds-barred theatrical spectacle can provide. When Mankind throws in his lot with World he puts on a robe festooned with gold coins (588, 701), a costume that both symbolically and realistically mirrors his decision. Backbiter runs around the playing area like a modern circus clown, carrying a little box which contains, he says, letters of defamation (673). Belyal rallies his troops for battle with smoke, fire, and blaring bagpipes, and during the fight the virtues pelt his forces with roses (2210–20). Flesh is on horseback (1940) when he marshals his allies for battle, and they carry a variety of weapons that are both realistic and symbolic. Gluttony has a firebrand; Lechery carries a pot of burning coals; Sloth has a spade. Other combatants are equally well armed. Anger has stones and a crossbow; Envy is armed with a bow; most carry shields and banners.

The play's circular stage design demands a great deal of physical movement from the actors—a dynamic contrast to the static, abstract quality of the conceptual allegory presented in their speeches—and another source of theatrical vividness. Five scaffolds surround the circular playing area, and as the plot of the play unfolds, the characters move from one scaffold to another, or to the castle in the center. This constantly moving focus of interest—similar in effect to a series of cut shots that jump from scene to scene in a modern motion picture—quickens the pace of the performance. As they circle the stage, some of the characters deliver theatrical asides to the surrounding audience—much like circus clowns moving around the ring of the circus—creating a close, even personal interrelationship that further deemphasizes the characters' abstract quality (550–52, 633 ff., 640 ff). Characters not assigned to any one scaffold; for instance, Mankind, Backbiter, and Death apparently move completely around the circle while they deliver their speeches of introduction, and at various points in the action, Backbiter dashes from one scaffold to another carrying messages.[5]

Elements of bourgeois realism typical of the medieval fabliaux—homely proverbs, highly perceptual similes (often drawn from domestic life), and vulgar, even gross, epithets—are scattered through the speeches of the play. Good Angel speaks of World's weal failing and fading like fish in the sea (353–54); World says he hops like a hawk in his fine mansion (458), and later that Mankind shouldn't "give a louse" for death (768–69). Bad Angel invites his good counterpart to "come blow at my nether end" (813–14); Devil says that when Mankind is dead he will bind him in hell "as catte dothe þe mows [mouse]" (951–52), and Mankind, when still in sin says, "I am no day wel . . . tyl I haue wel fyllyd my mawe" (1163–64). When Mankind complains that Confession has come too soon, Confession responds that before she comes again Mankind may long be in the grave with the toads and frogs (1360–61). Chastity says that the Lord made no room for Lust "whanne his blod strayed in þe strete" (2305), and in a comic blast at all the virtues, Bad Angel says that wherever women are there are many words (2649) and then adds, "Þer ges syttyn [where geese sit] are many tordys" (2651).

A characteristically realistic and comic exchange occurs after Sloth has been defeated in battle by industry. Sloth complains of the pain, and Bad Angel responds.

SLOTH

Out, I eye! ley on watyr!	[throw on water]
I swone, I swete, I feynt, I drulle!	[swoon; sweat; faint; drool]
ȝene qwene wyth hyr pytyr-patyr	[pitter-patter]
Hath al to-dayschyd my skallyd skulle.	[dashed to pieces; scabby]
It is as softe as wulle.	[wool]
Or I haue here more skathe,	[before; harm]
I schal lepe awey, be lurkynge lathe,	[leap; by a secret path]
Þere I may my ballokys bathe	[bathe my testicles]
And leykyn at þe fulle.	[play to the fullest]

BAD ANGEL

ȝa, þe Deuyl spede ȝou, al þe packe!	[take you; the whole pack]
For sorwe I morne on þe mowle,	[sorrow; earth, ground]
I carpe, I crye, I coure, I kacke,	[complain; cower; shit]
I frete, I fart, I fesyl fowle.	[fret; fart; fizzle foully]
I loke lyke an howle.	[look like an owl]

(2396–2409)

As we might expect, the evil characters in the play speak the more crude, vulgar, and comic lines, but speeches of the virtuous characters also include realistic and homely similes, proverbs, and metaphors, since the author obviously wanted to give all the characters in the play a share in the decorative realism that so appealed to fifteenth-century taste.[6]

But for all the vivid tomfoolery and detailed realism, the play depends just as heavily on the second side of the flamboyant duality—the ornate use of allegory, symbolism, repetition, and the other rhetorical schemes and figures of sound and meaning. Most of the play's 318 stanzas have a highly complex and ornate arrangement of rhyme, meter, and meaning. The most frequently recurring stanza type (235 out of 318) has thirteen lines; the second major type (45 out of 318) has nine; the remaining 38 stanzas range in length from two to fourteen lines.

By the extensive use of amplification and repetition most of the thirteen- and nine-line stanzas arrange their meanings into a two-part division.[7] The first part of most thirteen-line stanzas presents two closely related statements, the second statement usually expanding and elaborating upon the general sense of the first; the first part of each nine-line stanza presents a single statement; the second part of both the nine- and thirteen-line stanzas restates and concludes the basic sense presented in the first part, generally adding some new idea or twist of meaning. With only a few exceptions, this concluding restatement is contained in the last four lines of both stanza types and is marked off from the first part of each by a distinct change in the rhythm and rhyme schemes.

This patterning of sound and meaning within the stanzas imposes a limit on what and how much the poet can say in each stanza, since the pattern he sets up only permits the initial statement to be developed or amplified and then concluded, in most cases limiting the addition of any new ideas not closely related to those contained in the initial statement. In the thirteen-line stanzas the first four lines present an initial statement, the next five lines develop and amplify this statement, and the final four lines restate and conclude the initial idea. In the nine-line stanzas, the pattern is essentially the same, without the middle section of development and amplification. The initial statement, with some elaboration and development occurs in the first five lines, and the last four lines provide the restatement and conclusion.

In each of the nine- and thirteen-line stanzas this two-part division of meaning is accompanied and signaled by, as I have said, a change in rhythm and rhyme which both sets off the final four-line conclusion from the rest of the stanza and links the two sections together, since the last line in the first half

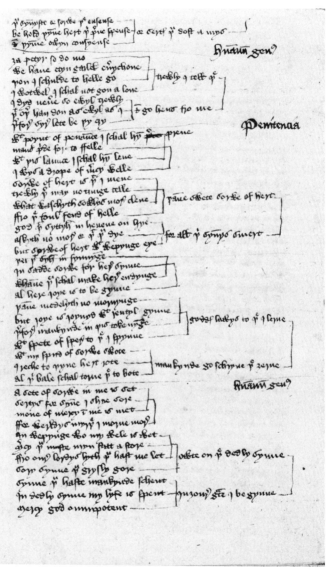

7. Folio 191, verso, the Macro Manuscript. By permission of the Folger Shakespeare Library

40

of each stanza rhymes with the last line of the conclusion. In the manuscript, the scribe drew attention to this division by separating these two lines from the other lines in each stanza (see Figure 7). The rhyme scheme in the majority of thirteen-line stanzas is: 1) *a b a b a b a b c*/ 2) *d d d c*. In most nine-line stanzas the pattern is essentially the same: 1) *a b a b c*/ 2) *d d d c*. Although neither the number of syllables nor the number of stresses in each line is consistent from one stanza to another, the number is always reduced in the second part of each stanza, though the amount of reduction is also variable.

The following stanzas are typical of the poet's practice. The first, spoken by Flesh, illustrates the thirteen-line pattern; the second, spoken by Mankind, is typical of the nine-line pattern.

FLESH

I byde as a brod brustun-gutte abouyn on þese tourys.	a	
Euerybody is þe betyr þat to myn byddynge is bent.	b	
I am Mankyndys fayre Flesch, florchyd in flowrys.	a	[*First half:*
My lyfe is wyth lustys and lykynge ilent.	b	*statement*
Wyth tapytys of tafata I tymbyr my towrys.	a	*and*
In myrthe and in melodye my mende is iment.	b	*expan-*
Þou I be clay and clad, clappyd vndir clowrys,	a	*sion*]
Ʒyt wolde I þat my wyll in þe werld went,	b	
Full trew I ʒou behyth.	c	
I loue wel myn ese,	d	[*Conclud-*
In lystys me to plese;	d	*ing re-*
Þou synne my sowle sese	d	*state-*
I ʒeue not a myth.	c	*ment*]
		(235–47)

The idea that Flesh doesn't give a mite if sin seizes his soul is the additional twist of meaning presented in the conclusion.

MANKIND

ȝa, Petyr, so do mo!	a
We haue etyn garlek euerychone.	b [*First half:*
Þou I schulde to helle go,	a *initial statement*]
I wot wel I schal not gon alone,	b
Trewly I tell þe.	c
I dyd neuere so ewyl trewly	d
But oþyr han don as ewyl as I.	d [*Concluding*
Þerfore, syre, lete be þy cry	d *restatement*]
And go hens fro me.	c

(1368–76)

In this stanza, the last two lines present the additional twist of meaning—a request that Confession, to whom Mankind is speaking, stop talking and leave him alone.

This complex arrangement of meaning, syntax, rhyme, meter, and alliteration in each stanza is typical flamboyant ornamentation. The repetitive pattern of each stanza retards the flow of ideas, the decorative sound structure draws attention to itself, and neither serves any apparent rhetorical purpose. Clearly the decoration is introduced for its own sake, because the poet and his audience enjoy it.

Aureate, that is, golden terms—words of French or Latin derivation—also embellish the stanzas with their rhythmic, multisyllabic, sonorous, or uncommon quality.[8] Compared to the other two plays in the Macro manuscript, *The Castle of Perseverance* makes only sparing use of aureate diction. When such words do appear, they come in clusters, usually in rhyme position, and most often in the speeches of the virtuous characters.

Sixty-one Latin phrases scattered throughout the various speeches offer another kind of verbal ornamentation. Some of these are integrated by rhyme and meter into the stanzas where they occur; others stand apart from the stanza. All but a few of them simply restate what already is said in English, their presence not required for sense. Like the aureate terms in this play, most of the Latin phrases are spoken either by one of the virtuous characters or by Mankind. In fact, thirty-three of the sixty-one appear in the final 420-line scene where God and the Four Daughters of God talk in heaven. A medieval Catholic audience could not have imagined a more fitting ornament for heavenly conversation than the use of Latin. Some of the Latin phrases are direct quotations from the Bible, and by adding an aura of scriptural authority, may have increased the dramatic impact of the speeches in which they occur.[9]

The poet made extensive use of one further ornament—the sequential arrangement of stanzas into balanced symmetrical patterns. Since as a rule each individual character speaks a complete stanza (a few stanzas are divided between two characters), the overall effect of these stanza groups is not just verbal symmetry but an arrangement of the characters who speak them into elaborate visual and aural tableaux. The play opens with a sequence of oratorical displays by Mankind's three major enemies: World, Devil, and Flesh, each rhetorically ornate and symmetrically balanced verbal fanfares. When the three have completed their self descriptions, Mankind enters and explains his spiritual and physical frailty in the four-stanza expository speech.

Stanza	Speaker	Number of Lines
1	World	13
2	World	13
3	World	13
4	Devil	13
5	Devil	13
6	Devil	13

Stanza	Speaker	Number of Lines
7	Flesh	13
8	Flesh	13
9	Flesh	14
10	Mankind	13
11	Mankind	13
12	Mankind	13
13	Mankind	13

The equal number of stanzas spoken by World, Devil, and Flesh (Flesh's fourteen-line stanza serves no significant purpose) signals the equivalent strength and importance of the three characters. The four stanzas delivered by Mankind not only vary the pattern, and so avoid monotony, but also serve a more important theatrical purpose. World, Devil, and Flesh delivered their speeches of introduction from scaffolds and would have had no difficulty being heard by all of the audience in the circular theatre. But Mankind has no such scaffold assigned to him, and so he must speak these four stanzas from the grass or central playing place, probably delivering them processionally while circling the arena, so that everyone in the audience can see and hear him, unobstructed by the castle in the center.

After Mankind has introduced himself, he immediately engages in a debate with Good and Bad Angel about the moral direction his life should take. The sequence is like a legal disputation and it is carefully balanced among the three participants. Mankind decides in favor of Bad Angel, who speaks one stanza more than Good Angel in the debate, and Good Angel closes the sequence with a stanza of lament.

Stanza	Speaker	Number of Lines
14	Good Angel	13
15	Bad Angel	9
16	Good Angel	13
17	Bad Angel	13
18	Mankind	9
19	Bad Angel	9
20	Mankind	9
21	Good Angel	9
22	Bad Angel	9
23	Mankind	9
24	Bad Angel	9
25	Mankind	9
26	Good Angel	9 [lament]

When he has won the debate, Bad Angel introduces Mankind to World, and after Mankind has pledged himself to be World's true servant he is taken to be clothed in fine array by two of World's knights. This symbolically meaningful costume change most likely occurs offstage; at any rate, the break in the action that the change requires is filled by the self-introduction of Backbiter, World's page. Like Mankind, Backbiter enters the circular arena on the grass and most probably delivers his four stanzas processionally.[10]

The next balanced grouping of stanzas comes shortly after this. Mankind has reentered, clothed in his coin-studded robe, and is sent by World to the scaffold of his treasurer, Sir Covetous. After Backbiter introduces them, Covetous welcomes Mankind and describes his own attributes. This speech is parallel in purpose and scope to the introductory speeches of World, Flesh, and Devil at the start of the play, and as we might expect in this balanced structure, it is three thirteen-line stanzas long.

After Covetous's greeting and self-explanation, he calls on the other deadly sins to come over to his scaffold and teach Mankind the ways of evil. The action shifts first to the scaffold of Devil and then to Flesh's scaffold as each of the three sins assigned to these powers takes his leave and heads off to Covetous's scaffold. At the end of each sequence, first Devil and then Flesh bid their three allies farewell. Like the structure of each stanza, this sequence is in two parts, the second part a structural repetition of the first.

Stanza	Speaker	Number of Lines
66	Pride	13
67	Anger	13
68	Envy	13
69	Devil	13
70	Gluttony	13
71	Lechery	13
72	Sloth	13
73	Flesh	13

The action of the play now shifts back to Covetous's scaffold as the six sins arrive and, with Covetous, complete the gathering of all seven deadly sins. There is some introductory greeting, then each sin instructs Mankind in his particular lore and Mankind embraces one after the other, affirming his intention to use each sin in his life. This neatly structured sequence, accompanied by repetition of action as each sin instructs Mankind and then accepts Mankind's invitation to join him on Covetous's scaffold, symbolically presents Mankind's willful commitment to a life in sin. The only variation in the pattern comes at the beginning, where Pride, traditionally considered the root of other sins, delivers two boastful stanzas describing himself.

Stanza	Speaker	Number of Lines
77	Pride	13
78	Pride	13
79	Mankind	13
80	Pride and Mankind	4
81	Anger	13
82	Mankind	13
83	Anger and Mankind	4
84	Envy	13
85	Mankind	13
86	Envy and Mankind	4
87	Gluttony	13
88	Mankind	13
89	Gluttony and Mankind	4
90	Lechery	13
91	Mankind	13
92	Lechery and Mankind	4
93	Sloth	13
94	Mankind	13
95	Sloth and Mankind	4

At the close of this ornately balanced, repetitive sequence, Mankind, already pledged to Covetous, is a confirmed sinner. The stanzaic patterning and symbolic action give a ponderous dignity and solemnity to this important point in the action, and this tone is sustained when Confession and Penitence arrive. These two have been summoned by a lament from Good

Angel, and after some delay and resistance on Mankind's part, they lead him back into the state of Grace and introduce him to the seven virtues, antidotes to the seven sins. A leaf is missing from the manuscript at this point, but the stanzaic grouping, though incomplete, is clear. In the pattern established, each Virtue introduces herself to Mankind in a single thirteen-line stanza. Five of the seven remain.

Mankind is next led into the castle of perseverance to take both symbolic and realistic refuge from the onslaught of temptation. Bad Angel quickly brings the news of Mankind's repentance to Backbiter, who then carries it to each of the three powers of evil. The sequence is pure farce, or circus. When Backbiter brings the news first to Devil, then to Flesh and World, each calls his chief sin and berates him for allowing Mankind to escape to a virtuous life. As Backbiter gleefully comments on the action, each of the sins is beaten by his master and each promises to get Mankind back if only the beating will stop. The stanzas are again arranged in a symmetrically repetitive series that moves the action around the circular arena so everyone gets a chance to see at least one sequence. The only two structural variations are the use of nine lines instead of thirteen in stanzas 139 and 154.

Stanza	Speaker	Number of Lines
139	Backbiter	9
140	Backbiter	4
141	Devil	4
142	Backbiter	13
143	Pride	2
144	Devil	9
145	Backbiter	13
146	Backbiter	4

Stanza	Speaker	Number of Lines
147	Flesh	4
148	Backbiter	13
149	Lechery	2
150	Flesh	9
151	Backbiter	13
152	Backbiter	4
153	World	4
154	Backbiter	9
155	Covetous	2
156	World	9

When this comic sequence ends, the evil forces prepare to besiege the castle and win Mankind back to a life of sin. After some stanzas of exhortation on both sides, with Bad Angel spurring on the forces of evil and Good Angel exhorting the virtues, the siege begins. The actual battle is a stylistically flamboyant combination of realistic theatrical activity and decorative tableaux, since the stanza patterning creates stylized groupings of characters that contrast sharply with the stage business of the fighting. The battle is in two parts; first the three sins under Devil's command fight with their counterparts, then Flesh's three sins fight with their opposing virtues. Covetous, the one sin under World's direction, avoids a physical fight with Generosity, ending the sequence with a twist of reference similar to that found at the end of each two-part stanza structure. After their stanzas of response, Humility, Patience, and Charity pelt their opposition with roses. The text gives no clear indication what Abstinence, Chastity, and Industry do in battle, though Lechery speaks as if Chastity has used a bucket of water to quench the fires of lust (2388–90).

49

Stanza	Speaker	Number of Lines
173	Devil	9 [exhortation]
174	Pride	13 [challenge]
175	Humility	13 [response]
176	Humility	13 [response]
177	Anger	13 [challenge]
178	Patience	13 [response]
179	Patience	13 [response]
180	Envy	13 [challenge]
181	Charity	13 [response]
182	Charity	13 [response]
183	Devil	13 [exhortation]

Stage direction: "Tunc pugnabunt diu [Then they fight for a long while]."

Stanza	Speaker	Number of Lines
184	Pride	9 [cry of defeat]
185	Envy	9 [cry of defeat]
186	Anger	9 [cry of defeat]
187	Bad Angel	9 [comment]
188	Flesh	13 [exhortation]
189	Gluttony	13 [challenge]
190	Abstinence	13 [response]
191	Abstinence	13 [response]
192	Lechery	13 [challenge]
193	Chastity	13 [response]
194	Chastity	13 [response]
195	Sloth	13 [challenge
196	Industry	13 [response]
197	Industry	13 [response]
198	Flesh	13 [exhortation]

Stage direction: "Tunc pugnabunt diu
[Then they fight for a long while]."

199	Gluttony	9 [cry of defeat]
200	Lechery	9 [cry of defeat]
201	Sloth	9 [cry of defeat]
202	Bad Angel	9 [comment]
203	World	13 [exhortation]
204	Covetous	13 [speaks to Mankind]
205	Generosity	13 [response]
206	Generosity	13 [response]

The pattern is broken at this point when Covetous says to
Generosity, "What eylyth þe, Lady . . . I spak ryth [right] not to
þe,/ Þerfore I prey þe holde þi pes" (2466–69). He resumes his
conversation with Mankind, ignoring Generosity completely,
and after a measured, six-stanza debate, in which they each
speak three stanzas, Covetous persuades Mankind to leave the
castle and return to a life of sin. By this clever twist of the pattern, a Vice triumphs by rhetorically beguiling Mankind rather
than by defeating a Virtue.

Good Angel laments this second fall from grace and each of
the seven Virtues delivers a single stanza putting the blame on
Mankind's free will. At the end of these stanzas, Bad Angel
mocks the Virtues' dismay at their loss of Mankind; Mankind
restates his intention to follow Covetous; Good Angel again
laments Mankind's decision, and World gloats over his re-
newed good fortune. Then, in a second alternating sequence of
six stanzas like the one before, Covetous instructs Mankind in
the sin of avarice.

But Mankind's greed cannot protect him from the coming of
Death, and Death does come, entering on the grass and apparently delivering five stanzas processionally like the introductory stanzas spoken by Mankind and Backbiter earlier. Unlike

these other two processional speeches, this one is addressed directly to a character in the play rather than to the audience, and thus requires one more stanza—four to take Death around the full circle of the arena and the fifth delivered directly to Mankind, beginning with the line, "To Mankynde now wyl I reche." [11]

A series of unpatterned stanzas follows in which Mankind futilely calls for help from World, learns that his heir will be Garcio (or "boy," a total stranger), and finally dies in the state of sin, calling out for mercy. Mankind's soul then appears, berates the body, and after Good Angel laments the loss of Mankind's soul, Bad Angel gloats over this success and carries the soul off to hell on his back.

The final scene takes place in heaven and, as we've said, consists of a debate among the Four Daughters of God over the fate of Mankind's soul. The stanzas are again arranged symmetrically and organize the characters who speak them into a kind of heavenly *tableau vivant*.

Stanza	Speaker	Number of Lines
263	Mercy	13
264	Mercy	9
265	Justice	13
266	Justice	13
267	Truth	13
268	Truth	13
269	Peace	13
270	Peace	13
271	Truth	4
272	Mercy	4
273	Justice	4
274	Peace	4
275	God	4

In this sequence the characters introduce themselves and state their individual position about Mankind's eternal fate. They then go to the throne of God, and in the four-line stanzas each gives a greeting and says why she has come. God welcomes them and the debate is ready to begin at the throne of the Almighty. The change in speaking order in stanzas 271–74 seems a conscious device to break the potential monotony of an exact repetition and to establish the speaking order of the debate which now begins. Following parliamentary procedure, the debate sequence allows each of the disputants to present her case in turn.

Stanza	Speaker	Number of Lines
276	Truth	13
277	Truth	13
278	Truth	13
279	Truth	13
280	Truth	13
281	Mercy	13
282	Mercy	13
283	Mercy	13
284	Mercy	13
285	Mercy	13
286	Justice	13
287	Justice	13
288	Justice	13
289	Justice	13
290	Justice	13
291	Mercy	13
292	Mercy	13
293	Mercy	13
294	Peace	13
295	Peace	13

Stanza	Speaker	Number of Lines
296	Peace	13
297	Peace	13
298	Peace	13
299	Peace	13

With their extra stanzas, Mercy and Peace not only break the symmetry but also succeed in carrying the debate. God rules in their favor and sends all four to reclaim Mankind's soul from hell. In single stanzas of four lines each, the four express their concord and desire to obey God's command, and the play ends with four thirteen-line stanzas spoken by God welcoming Mankind to heavenly bliss and reaffirming that Mercy is triumphant over all. God's concluding speech is actually a little homily on eternal punishment and reward; it ends when the actor playing God abandons his dramatic character and directly addresses the audience to explain the moral of the play and praise God.

By grouping individually ornate stanzas into larger, balanced patterns, the author of *The Castle of Perseverance* creates an elaborate layered embellishment, much like the characteristic curves and countercurves—the circles within circles—which ultimately form the perfect circle of the rose windows of many fifteenth-century cathedrals. The result in this play, as in the architecture of the period, is an extreme heightening of ornamentation.

The play's style would have strongly appealed to audiences of the time. The blend of theatrical action, realistic language, costume detail, props, music, and spectacle with the extreme ornateness of the stanzas and stanza groupings, the elaborate allegory, and the symbolism creates the duality which is the essence of fifteenth-century flamboyance. Audiences would have especially noticed these matters of style as well as the various theatrical antics, since the meanings in the play—the allegory of the Vices and Virtues, their battle for the soul of man, the central place of the castle figure in this battle, the appearance of Death personified, the almost complete success of Covetous in subverting Mankind to sin, and the Debate of the Four Daughters of God—are basically derivative and offer little that would have been new or different apart from their flamboyant dramatization.

The play's handling of Death and his dance illustrates the extent to which it assumes the commonplaces of the period as givens. Here's how the character Death expresses the social doctrine that all men are equal in the face of death—a major and recurring aspect of the motif in lyrics, Dance of Death literature, and art in the fifteenth century. It's obviously the style, not the substance, that is important.

Dynge dukys arn adred	[*Worthy dukes are terrified*]
Whanne my blastys arn on hem blowe.	[*are on them blown*]
Lordys in londe arn ouyrled;	[*oppressed*]
Wyth þis launce I leye hem lowe.	[*lay them low*]
Kyngys kene and knytys kyd,	[*Mighty kings and renowned knights*]
I do hem deluyn in a throwe,	[*I pierce them in an instant*]
In banke I buske hem abed,	[*bring them quickly to the grave*]
Sad sorwe to hem I sowe,	[*them*]
I tene hem, as I trowe.	[*I vex them*]
As kene koltys þow þey kynse,	[*though they wince*]
Ageyns me is no defens.	
In þe grete pestelens	
Þanne was I wel knowe.	[*well known*]

(2804–16)

Later, when Mankind has died, Justice directly refers to the dance motif.

Vertuis he putte ful evyn away
Whanne Coveytyse gan hym avaunce.
He wende þat he schulde a levyd ay,   [*lived forever*]
Tyl Deth trypte hym on hys daunce,
  He loste hys wyttys fyve.

(3422–26)

But although the play's flamboyant style almost certainly delighted the fifteenth-century playgoer—and we'll see in the next chapters that the same can be said about *Mankind* and *Wisdom*—such evidence of popularity is an inadequate basis for an artistic judgment of each play, though it does provide important background information for such a judgment, particularly when the work is distant from us in time. In a completed literary structure, the stylistic features used in its composition function as formal elements, and a valid evaluation of the work must be based on how harmoniously such stylistic features fit together with all the other formal elements to create a structurally interrelated whole.

In *The Castle of Perseverance*, the complexities that result from the flamboyant ornamentation produce a number of repetitive two-part structures. There's a bipartite rhyme and rhythm pattern in the majority of stanzas, and a two-part arrangement of statement and restatement. The stanzas are spoken by dramatic characters who function on two levels, having both a theatrical and a conceptual or spiritual existence.

Many of the characters pair off symmetrically with one another. Every one of the seven sins has a virtuous opposite; there is a Good and a Bad Angel; Truth and Justice are paired with Mercy and Peace in the Debate scene; Flesh and Devil, each on a scaffold, and each with three sinful cohorts are perfectly balanced. World, whose one attendant sin, Covetous, has a scaffold to himself breaks the symmetry, but in doing so draws attention to this most pervasive of sins.

The stanza groupings often follow a two-part pattern as well, as one group echoes the arrangement of the group that has preceded it. The central battle scene functions this way, for instance. The fights of Flesh's and Devil's cohorts are analogous to the first statement/expansion section of the thirteen-line stanzas, and Covetous's victory operates analogously to the four-line conclusion with its additional twist of meaning. Together these stanza groupings create and support the total narrative structure or plot of the play—still another two-part structure.

The second part of the plot structure in *The Castle of Perseverance* serially restates the first part and adds a twist of meaning. Although the dramatic time within the play covers Mankind's entire life-span from birth to life after death, the events arranged by the plot deal only with Mankind's changes in moral fortune. The first part of the plot—from the beginning of the play to Mankind's entrance into the castle (154–1714)—is a unified action which presents Mankind's temptation, fall into sin, and repentance. The second part, or restatement, beginning with Bad Angel's vow that Mankind will not dwell long in the castle and continuing almost to the end of the play, when God welcomes Mankind to heaven (1715–3610), is also a unified structure with its own beginning, middle, and end serially presenting a second temptation and fall but ending with Mankind's eternal salvation rather than with a second repentance—a variation and conclusion to the plot's two-part repetitive structure. As the ultimate point toward which the action in both the first and second parts is directed, the salvation of Mankind serves to link the two parts together, giving a formal unity to the whole.

Speeches of Good and Bad Angel mark the points of division

in the plot structure in much the same way that rhyme and meter change function in the stanzas. The incidents depicting Mankind's first descent into sin are prefaced by a debate between the two angels and Good Angel's lament (446–55) that Mankind has forsaken him for a life of sin. At the end of this sequence of events Mankind is at his first moral nadir; the Good and Bad Angels again exchange comments about the incidents up to this point (1260–85), and Bad Angel boasts of his mastery over Mankind, thus emphasizing Mankind's collapse (1284–85).

The linear progression of incidents next shows Mankind's rise from the depths of this first fall into sin toward repentance and a life of virtue. This sequence begins with a speech by Good Angel who points out how completely Mankind has fallen into a life of sin and calls on God for mercy (1297). The cry is heard by Confession, and Mankind is led to reject sin and make a decision to live in virtue.

When Mankind has completed this first spiritual reversal and is safely housed in the castle of perseverance with the Virtues, the plot structure begins its repetition. As in the first part, the initial events of this second part trace Mankind's return to the depths of sin. This sequence is set in motion by Bad Angel in a stanza which begins, "Nay, be Belyals bryth [bright] bonys,/ Þer schal he no whyle dwelle" (1715–16). By the end of this sequence Mankind has reached his second moral collapse, signaled in a stanza spoken by Good Angel beginning, "Alas, þat euere Mankynde was born!/ On coueytyse is al hys lust" (2674–75). Mankind's second commitment to sin ends with a speech by Bad Angel who chides Mankind and finally carries his soul off to hell (3073–3128). Just before this occurs, however, Good Angel laments Mankind's fall and death in sin and affirms that Mankind is now beyond the help of all but God's mercy (3034–59). After Bad Angel has bid a comic farewell to the audience and departed for hell with Mankind's soul on his back, the debate of the Four Daughters of God begins, and from this point to the end of the play the two Angels are not seen or heard from again, having served their purpose both structurally and spiritually.

At each point in the play where Mankind's moral fortunes change direction, speeches by one or both of the Angels serve to motivate the change or to signal the end of a particular phase of Mankind's moral condition. By thus foregrounding the points of reversal and repetition in the plot's progression, the two Angels draw special attention to its two-part structure.

Although it was accepted doctrine that each human being had an angel guardian assigned to him, and that at the will of God bad angels or demons could tempt men,[12] there's no indication in medieval theology that each man has a good and a bad angel permanently assigned to him as attendant spirits. Yet, this is exactly what Mankind says when he introduces the Angels.

To aungels bene asynyd to me:	[*two; have been assigned*]
Þe ton techyth me to goode;	[*the one*]
On my ryth syde ȝe may hym se;	[*right*]
He cam fro Criste þat deyed on rode.	[*who died on the cross*]
Anoþyr is ordeynyd her to be	[*here*]
Þat is my foo, be fen and flode;	[*everyplace*]
He is about in euery degre	[*active; in every way*]
To drawe me to þo dewylys wode	[*those devils wild*]
Þat in helle ben thycke.	[*who are numerous in hell*]
	(301–9)

By creating Bad Angel, the poet clearly stretched accepted theological doctrine about angels in order to establish a foil for Good Angel and produce one more balanced pair for theatrical effect and structural signaling inside the fiction of the play.

Having paired them off neatly for structural purposes, the poet then expands the role of the two Angels to create a secondary story interest parallel to the one involving Mankind. The plot proceeds on two interwoven levels, tracing the falling-rising/ falling-rising pattern of Mankind's moral fortunes in terms of the success-failure/ success-failure pattern of the two Angels, whose respective good and bad fortunes accompany those of Mankind. This secondary interest draws additional attention to the points of reversal and repetition in the plot.

Because the plot turns back on itself, replaying in its second part the major incidents of its first part, a double circular structure (see Figure 8) is created from a basically linear arrangement of events. The plot of *The Castle of Perseverance* displays a tension of two contrasting principles—linearity and circularity—and borrowing a term used to describe the stone tracery of fifteenth-century cathedral windows, might be called

8. Design of *The Castle of Perseverance*. Original drawing by Robert Hickey

9. Stained-glass window at Canterbury Cathedral

curvilinear. Its incidents are serially related to one another by a principle of cause and effect but ultimately interrelated by a principle of bipartite, echoic repetition similar in form to the numerous other two-part structures in the play.

This elaborate, repetitive design is a ponderous and rhetorically inefficient way to present the play's commonplace doctrines and motifs and suggests that those elements were considered secondary to the ornate style and structure. We can see the same effect in one of the fifteenth-century windows at Canterbury Cathedral (see Figure 9), where the religious significance—the meaning—of the individual scenes is subordinate to the decorative tracery that surrounds and connects them. The religious rhetoric of the play would have been further subordinated in theatrical performance by the visual and aural impact of actors, voices, stage business, music and song, color, costuming, sets, props, and spectacle. It seems fair to conclude that the playwright was more concerned with design than with doctrinal substance—more anxious to produce a decorative dramatization than a dramatized sermon.

And a decorative dramatization—an ornate theatrical spectacle—is exactly what the playwright did produce. *The Castle of Perseverance* is a marvelous theatre piece, massive yet tightly controlled, bulky yet cleverly balanced. Its 3,600 lines contain realism and allegory, comedy and tragedy, moral doctrine and sexual vulgarity, spectacle and poetry, serious exposition and farcical dramatic action. These heterogeneous and normally incompatible elements are ordered and harmonized by the pervasive two-part design that touches each structural component in the play and similarly arranges the dissimilar elements. The various structural elements complement and reflect each other because each shares in the same principle of design, and all function together despite their differences to create a massive yet precise and finely tuned whole that is symmetrical and consistent, even musical in its harmony. Because of its harmonious consistency, the structure of *The Castle of Perseverance* is aesthetically pleasing, attracting our attention away from the commonplace message to its form as a well-ordered, sophisticated work of flamboyant art.

Chapter 3
Exposition and Illustration
Mankind

Compared to the balanced, harmonious form of *The Castle of Perseverance*, *Mankind* seems at first a disorganized, even sloppy, play. There's so much surface texture—in characterization, comedy, stage business, bawdy language, social commentary—that we can easily miss its organizing design. But on closer inspection we find that *Mankind* is a structurally complex and cleverly made play. It will be useful to begin with a brief summary of the action.

Mercy opens the play, introduces himself, laments Mankind's sinful condition, and tells the audience how to avoid temptation. Next, Mischief, Newguise, Nowadays, and Nought interrupt Mercy, tease him about his fancy language, then leave, and allow him to resume his exposition. After 185 lines, or almost 20 percent of the play, Mankind enters in the state of grace and urges the audience to be attentive to Mercy's advice. Mercy resumes his instruction, is again interrupted by the rogues, but finally finishes his sermon, warns Mankind about the devil Titivillus, and departs. Newguise, Nowadays, and Nought now enter and tempt Mankind to sin, but he is strong in his resolve, and routs the three. The rogues complain to Mischief, and he calls on Titivillus who successfully persuades Mankind to abandon work, prayer, and hope and embrace a life of sin. Mischief next sets up a mock manorial court where Mankind swears his allegiance to various sinful ways. After some comic horseplay, Mercy enters and tries to persuade Mankind to repent. Mankind at first rejects him, but when he learns later that Mercy is still looking for him, Mankind despairs and tries to hang himself. Mercy reenters just in time to prevent the hanging and drives off the rogues; Mankind is restored to grace, and the play ends as Mercy delivers a final warning sermon to the audience.

Mankind is a relatively late fifteenth-century work (ca. 1467) and highly flamboyant. Mercy's lengthy sermonizing at the beginning of the play and his speeches throughout are loaded with abstract language, rhetorical colors and figures, and aureate diction—standard ornaments of the high style that, as we've seen, forms one side of the typical flamboyant duality.

The very fownder and begynner of owr fyrst creacyon
Amonge ws synfull wrechys he oweth to be magnyfyede,
Þat for owr dysobedyenc he hade non indygnacyon
To sende hys own son to be torn and crucyfyede.
Owr obsequyouse seruyce to hym xulde be aplyede,   [*should*]
Where he was lorde of all and made all thynge of nought,
For þe synnfull synnere to hade hym revyuyde   [*revived*]
And for hys redempcyon sett hys own son at nought.

Yt may be seyde and veryfyede, mankynde was dere bought.
By þe pytuose deth of Jhesu he hade hys remedye.

He was purgyde of hys defawte þat wrechydly hade wrought
By hys gloryus passyon, þat blyssyde lauatorye.
O souerence, I beseche yow yowr condycyons to rectyfye
Ande wyth hymylite and reuerence to haue a remocyon
To þis blyssyde prynce þat owr nature doth gloryfye,
Þat ʒe may be partycypable of hys retribucyon.

(1–16)[1]

The most striking feature of these two opening stanzas is their encrusted verbal decoration. In the first line of each stanza, aureate terms pair off with common Anglo-Saxon synonyms in order to attract more attention to themselves: "fownder and begynner," "seyde and veryfyede." The sole concrete image in the entire sixteen lines is the phrase "torn and crucyfyede" in line three. The bulk of this and Mercy's other speeches consists of abstractions, often set in repetitive groupings like "fyrst creacyon," "obsequyouse seruyce," and "synnfull synnere," designed to embellish the tone of high learning. Mercy's speeches frequently make use of decorative metaphors and a wide variety of other rhetorical ornaments. The passion of Christ is called a "blyssyde lauatorye" in line thirteen. A little further on that metaphor turns up again linked this time with a simile.

I mene Owr Sauyowr, þat was lykynnyde to a lambe;
Ande hys sayntys be þe members þat dayly he doth satysfye
Wyth þe precyose reuer þat runnyth from hys wombe.   [*river*]

Ther ys non such foode, be water nor by londe,
So precyouse, so gloryouse, so nedefull to owr entent,
For yt hath dyssoluyde mankynde from þe bytter bonde
Of þe mortall enmye, þat vemynousse serpente,
From þe wyche Gode preserue yow all at þe last jugement!

(34–41)

Here rhetorical figuration—repetition, metaphor, simile, metonymy, and aureate diction—all add decoration to Mercy's speech. The series "so precyouse, so gloryouse, so nedefull to owr entent" balances these short parallel phrases to produce a crescendo of sound and meaning. It's clear enough that the audience is supposed to notice all of this. When interrupted by Mischief in the midst of his opening speech, Mercy responds "Avoyde, goode broþer! ȝe ben culpable / To interrupte thus my talkyng delectable" (64–65). A little later Newguise says to Mercy, "Ey, ey! yowr body ys full of Englysch Latin. / I am aferde yt wyll brest [burst]" (124–25).

Whereas the poet's practice in *The Castle of Perseverance* is to assign a full stanza to each speaker, the *Mankind* poet often splits stanzas between speakers, quickening the pace of the dialogue but eliminating the chance to arrange speakers by stanza groupings for further decoration. To achieve additional stylistic embellishment this poet carefully adjusts the sound structure to characterization. When alone, Mercy speaks in eight-line stanzas rhyming *a b a b b c b c*, with an interlocking rhyme. When Mercy and Mankind share scenes they speak in four-line stanzas—sixty-four in all—rhyming *a b a b*. In contrast, Mischief, Newguise, Nowadays, and Nought speak in eight-line stanzas—fifty-seven of them—with a simpler, less dignified tail rhyme. Fifty-five of these stanzas rhyme *a a a b c c c b*, and two, *a a a b a a a b*.

The author similarly adjusts the meter of the stanzas to fit characterization. Mercy and Mankind speak in fairly consistent four-stress lines in contrast to Mischief and the others, whose speeches have highly varied rhythms and an inconsistent number of stresses to the line. The uneven meter reinforces the characterization of the rogues as rude and rough fellows when compared to the more formal and lyrical meter used by Mankind in grace and Mercy.

Mankind's diction mirrors his spiritual state in much the same way. His opening lines, spoken when he is in the state of grace, make considerable use of aureate terms, abstract nouns, and static verbs.

Of þe erth and of þe cley we haue owr propagacyon.   [*clay*]
By þe prouydens of Gode þus be we deryvatt,   [*providence*]
To whos mercy I recomende þis holl congrygacyon: [*whole*]
I hope onto hys blysse ye be all predestynatt.

(186–89)

Mankind's language remains suitably ornate until he falls into sin when it becomes noticeably less elegant. In response to Mercy's request that he leave the rogues' company, he says:

I xall speke wyth þe anoþer tyme, to-morn,   [*shall*]
   or þe next day.
We xall goo forth together to kepe my
   faders ʒer-day.   [*anniversary of a death*]
A tapster, a tapster! stow, statt, stow!

(727–29)

At the end of the play, when he has returned to the state of grace, Mankind again uses aureate and abstract terms.

O Mercy, my suavius solas and synguler   [*sweet; source of comfort*]
   recreatory,
My predilecte spesyall, ʒe are worthy to   [*beloved; you*]
   hawe my lowe;
For wythowte deserte and menys   [*means*]
   supplicatorie
ʒe be compacient to my inexcusabyll   [*compassionate*]
   reprowe.

(871–74)

Latin words and phrases used by all the characters, good and evil, add further ornamentation. The tonal range of Latin usage is wide, extending from Mankind's "Memento, homo, quod cinis es et in cinerem reverteris [Remember man that you are dust, and unto dust you will return]" (Job 34:15) to Nought's "osculare fundamentum [kiss my ass]." It includes the Lord's Prayer, spoken by Mankind, as well as a quote by Newguise from the Psalms, "Cum sancto sanctus eris et cum perverso perverteris [With the holy you will be holy, and with the wicked you will be wicked]" (18:25–26). The effect is sometimes comic, sometimes serious, occasionally bawdy, but always ornamental. Brief references to popular allegorical motifs of the fifteenth century also decorate the play. These include, for instance, the battle of the vices and virtues (323–412), the debate of the body and soul (186–212), the Four Daughters of God (839–42), the coming of Death (736, 861–66), and the World, Flesh, and Devil as Mankind's major spiritual enemies (879–90).

Various forms of stylistic realism produce the other side of *Mankind*'s flamboyant duality. The hero, Mankind, who as a type character represents all men, is particularized here as a farmer with spade, a sack of seed, and the job of turning the earth to prepare it for planting. *Mankind* is the only morality play in the Macro group to assign a profession to its hero and to show him at work; we also see him as he prays and sleeps. The poet heightens our sense of Mankind as one specific man among many, rather than a type representing all men, by having Newguise, Nowadays, and Nought recite a catalogue of other men's names and hometowns when Titivillus sends them off to rob and riot.

NEW GYSE. Fyrst I xall begyn at Master Huntyngton of Sauston,
Fro thens I xall go to Wylliam Thurlay of Hauston,

Ande so forth to Pycharde of Trumpyngton.
I wyll kepe me to þes thre.
NOWADAYS. I xall goo to Wyllyham Baker of Waltom,
To Rycherde Bollman of Gayton;
I xall spare Master Woode of Fullburn,
He ys a noli me tangere.   [*someone to be left alone*]

NOUGHT. I xall goo to Wyllyam Patryke of Massyngham,
I xall spare Master Alyngton of Botysam
Ande Hamonde of Soffenham,

                                            (505–15)

The text doesn't tell us who these people are—William Baker
of Waltom, and so on—but clearly these are names of real people, and possibly the actors substituted different names from
performance to performance and town to town. Perhaps they
were local citizens who had been robbed, vandalized, or otherwise victimized, but in any case the catalogue adds particularity—another form of decorative realism—and emphasizes
Mankind's individuality.

Homely realism reminiscent of the bourgeois fabliau appears
throughout the play, especially in scenes featuring the rogues.
There are vulgar similes: "Þe Deull may daunce in my purse for
ony peny;/ Yt ys as clen as a byrdys ars" (488–89); specific
images: "I haue a lytyll dyshes [disease], as yt plesse Gode to
sende,/ Wyth a runnynge ryngeworme" (629–30); and even a
vulgar Christmas song on the topic of personal hygiene after
bowel movements (335–43)—a song punning on the words
"hole" and "holy" and ending as a raunchy parody of the
"Sanctus" or "Holy, Holy, Holy" of the Mass. At one point,
Newguise complains that his wife is his master and says that
because of her he has a bandage on his head, "Ande anoþer þer
[where] I pysse" (248). The poor fellow is left completely undone after Mankind routs all three rogues by bashing them
with his spade (376 ff.); Nowadays is struck in the head,

Nought in the arm, and Newguise moans that his testicles have been grievously injured (429, 430, 441). The three complain again about these injuries to Titivillus and ask him to get revenge on Mankind (496–98). There is even a medieval version of the still current epithet when Newguise tells Mankind "I wolde yowr mowth and hys ars . . . wer maryede junctly [married jointly] together" (346–47).

Unlike *The Castle of Perseverance*, where much of the realism is grounded in verbal description, costuming, and the homely proverbs, epithets, and oaths spoken by the various characters, *Mankind* presents realistic actions in addition to words. The characters in *Mankind* don't just perform actions linked to the abstract moral concept they stand for; they do other things onstage as well. Nought unceremoniously trips Mercy, bringing him to the ground (113), and the physical reality of the act is even more impressive because Mercy is such a dignified, abstraction-spouting character. Mankind leaves the stage and his prayers (561) to move his bowels, and Nought inadvertently empties his bowels on his own foot (784). The rogues play a game, "What how, ostlere, hostler! Lende ws [us] a football!" (732); and there is a surprisingly modern bit of stage business on the order of Laurel and Hardy —but more grim—when Newguise accidentally hangs himself while showing Mankind how to use a rope to commit suicide (808–10). Like all cartoon and slapstick characters, the rogues never appear to be genuinely hurt by their misadventures. As a result of these more humanly—or clownishly—real actions, *Mankind* seems to occur in "actual" time when compared to *The Castle of Perseverance* or *Wisdom* which handle time more symbolically, presenting only acts of moral decision making or demonstrations of moral failure.

Mankind is structured as a sermon with illustrative dramatizations, and its form allows and even encourages an action-based realism in the presentation of characters. Because they function to illustrate and exemplify what the sermon segments of the play expositorily present, the four evil rogues Mischief, Newguise, Nowadays, and Nought are imaginatively drawn, quasi-fictional characters who are only loosely identified with theological or doctrinal concepts outside the play itself. Mischief, for example, is far too generalized to be closely identified with any specific concept in the moral scheme. He may stand for all human sins, or he may be the ultimate result of sin—despair of salvation and the desire for suicide.[2] He is not Mankind's tempter in the play; Newguise, Nowadays, Nought, and Titivillus perform that function. Certainly Mischief is a foil or antagonist for Mercy, but that is a function inside the play and reveals little about his theological meaning—Justice would be the expected theological opposite of Mercy.

In much the same way, Newguise, Nowadays, and Nought are fictionally drawn attributes of World, one of man's three traditional enemies, but they are not World as such nor do they collectively stand for World. Thus they too are only tenuously linked to a doctrinal concept outside the play. The play encourages us to think of them as specific individuals rather than concrete presentations of abstract concepts—Nowadays has a wife named Rachel (135), Newguise is married to a shrew (246–52), and Nought plays the fool "wyth þe comyn tapster [barmaid] of Bury" (274). When Titivillus tells the three to take "William Fyde" (503) with them if they want another companion to help them rob and riot through the countryside, that too helps us think of them as three particular individuals.

Because they don't stand for a specific theological or moral idea outside the play, the rogues don't need to deliver long expository speeches of self-introduction like those provided by Mercy and Mankind. Mischief even neglects to state his own name during his first appearance onstage and, when he next appears, simply says, "I, Myscheff, was here at the begynnynge of þe game/ Ande arguyde wyth Mercy, Gode gyff hym schame!"

(417–18). Similarly, Newguise, Nowadays, and Nought merely recite their names when Mercy says, "Say me yowr namys, I know you not" (114).[3]

Unlike the other evil characters, Titivillus does stand for a spiritually real entity outside the play, but his characterization is more fictional than that of any other morality play devil— he comes across more like a comic magician than the Prince of Darkness. He provides hardly any self introduction, his costume and delayed but spectacular entrance probably sufficing to identify him clearly to the audience. Before he begins to tempt Mankind, he takes us into his confidence, discloses in advance what he will do, and explains that he can make himself invisible. He dashes offstage with the spade when Mankind throws it down in disgust but returns in the next moment and assures us that he has no lead on his heels (521–56). He teaches us a secret spell, and before he sneaks up on the sleeping Mankind to whisper temptations in his ear, he swears everyone in the audience to silence on pain of a forty-pence fine (590–91). He presents himself as Mankind's opponent in a game of chicanery rather than in a battle of good and evil, and when he has successfully brought Mankind from grace to sin, he bids us farewell and we never see or hear from him again: "Farewell, euerychon! for I haue don my game,/ For I haue brought Mankynde to myscheff and to schame" (605–6). His name, Titivillus, reinforces his relatively benign character, since it was traditionally used for the minor devil who gathered up scraps of mispronounced Latin in monastery choirs.[4] It's also an interesting choice for the name of the Devil in a play so thoroughly aware of language in its use of puns, aureate diction, and caustic satire of the clerical manner of speaking.

To a lesser extent, Mercy and Mankind share in the heightened theatrical realism that marks the presentation of the quasi-fictional forces of evil. Though Mankind and Mercy are fairly consistent presentations of doctrinal concepts outside the play, there are times when theatrical demands take over from the allegory and the two temporarily become particularized dramatic characters, cut free from their conceptual base. For example, Mercy doesn't always or only act merciful. He also functions as a father confessor—a priest or preacher—who teaches Mankind the means for salvation.[5] In his opening stanza, Mercy's use of "us" and "our" makes him sound like one of us—human and sinful—and blurs his characterization as an attribute of the Divine mind.

Amonge *ws* synfull wrechys he oweth to be magnyfyede,
Þat for *owr* dysobedyenc he hade non indygnacyon
To sende hys own son to be torn and crucyfyede.
Owr obsequyouse seruyce to hym xulde be aplyede,

(My italics; 2–5)

By line eighteen, however, he is clearer in his self-conception.

Mercy ys my name, þat mornyth for *yowr* offence.
Dyverte not *yowrsylffe* in tyme of temptacyon,
Þat ȝe may be acceptable to Gode at *yowr* goyng hence.

(My italics; 18–20)

But at line twenty-four he seems to have lost his identity again: "I prey Gode at yowr most nede þat mercy be yowr defendawnte."

When Mercy warns Mankind about the battle between the soul and body (227 ff.) and discusses the various earthly pleasures, he is characterized as a teacher not a personification of Mercy.

Mesure ys tresure. Y forbyde yow not þe vse.
Mesure yowrsylf euer; be ware of excesse.
Þe superfluouse gyse I wyll þat ȝe refuse,
When nature ys suffysyde, anon þat ȝe sese.

(237–40)

Later, near the end of the play, Mercy reviews his earlier warnings to Mankind and again assumes the role of teacher.

Mankend, ȝe were obliuyows of my doctrine monytorye.
I seyd before, Titiuillus wold asay ȝow a bronte.   [*attack*]
Be ware fro hensforth of hys fablys delusory.

(879–81)

These and other speeches like them in the play indicate that Mercy's characterization is something more than a purely allegorical presentation of God's mercy. The lessons he preaches and the points he makes are doctrinally valid, but they are not exclusively concrete illustrations of mercy.

Mankind's characterization, like Mercy's, shifts throughout the play. At some times he is an allegorical, or more precisely typological, character representing all humanity; at other times he presents himself as a particularized individual. The change in characterization often occurs within a single speech, signaled by a variation in the personal pronouns that Mankind uses. Mankind chooses the first person plural when he wants to include himself with the audience, but when he switches to the first person singular or second person plural, he effectively distances himself from the rest of humanity and presents himself as a separate individual, distinct from the mass of mankind. The inconsistency is particularly noticeable in Mankind's opening speech.

Of þe erth and of þe cley *we* haue *owr* propagacyon.
By þe prouydens of Gode þus be *we* deryvatt,
To whos mercy *I* recomende þis holl congrygacyon:
I hope onto hys blysse *ye* be all predestynatt.

Euery man for hys degre *I* trust xall be partycypatt,
Yf *we* wyll mortyfye *owr* carnall condycyon
Ande *owr* voluntarye dysyres, þat euer be pervercyonatt,
To renunce þem and yelde *ws* wnder Godys provycyon.

(My italics; 186–93)

In these two stanzas Mankind's characterization holds fairly consistently to that of a type character but ranges momentarily into an individual characterization. Later in the play he again reverts to the status of an individual when he asks the three rogues, "Have ʒe non other man to moke [mock], but ever me?" (378), and when he leaves to move his bowels: "I wyll into þe ʒerde, souerens, and cum ageyn son./ For drede of þe colyke and eke of þe ston/ I wyll go do þat nedys must be don" (561–63).

Inconsistencies in characterization like these make *Mankind* a far less "pure" allegorical drama than either of the other two Macro plays. Because the characters are not consistently allegorical, the play often seems as if it is about to burst out of its generic confines as a morality into something more akin to Renaissance comedy.

Though we could argue that the *Mankind* author was innovatively ahead of his time and that his play is a transitional piece, it's far more likely that the poet was so at ease with the allegorical mind-set of the fifteenth century—with the flamboyant duality—that his abstract characters could and did become more dramatically real, more individualized, in response to the requirements of the play's form as an illustrated sermon. We should probably view *Mankind* as an example of late, extreme flamboyance rather than as an early renaissance work.

Because it mixes allegorical and semifictional characters, the play is stylistically flamboyant on two levels simultaneously. On the one hand, concretely real stage characters present abstract concepts and the blend follows the general outline provided by the figure of allegory that we find in the other moralities. On the other hand, because the rogues are particular, fictionalized characters, and because at times even Mankind and Mercy become particularized as well, a second mixture of allegory and realism occurs as the play unfolds linearly and shifts from doctrinal exposition to illustrative dramatized examples, then back again to doctrinal exposition. The actions of Mercy and Mankind are usually controlled by the doctrinal system outside the play, whereas Newguise, Nowadays, Nought, Mischief, and even Titivillus, to some extent, are motivated in their actions as much from within the play as from the external abstract theological system which the play presents.

This double mixture of fiction and doctrine, realism and allegory, makes *Mankind* the most flamboyant of the three Macro moralities and in the process creates something like a hybrid genre. *Mankind* is not realistic comedy, but it is not a wholly typical morality play either, since some of its characters are more humanly real than allegorical. *Mankind* is an example of flamboyance gone wild, a mixture of styles each taken to its ultimate level of ornateness, threatening, but never completely breaking the synthesis into its two component parts.

As a counterbalance to its stylistic complexity, *Mankind* has surprisingly simple production requirements. The play's manuscript contains no stage plan or detailed list of props and costumes, but we can infer from the text what the production and the circumstances surrounding it were like. The cast was small; the play requires no more than six male actors, if the same actor doubles as both Mercy and Titivillus.[6] (There is singing and dancing in the play, necessitating more than one musician—Newguise says, "Ande how, mynstrellys, pley þe comyn trace!" [72]—but the musicians may well have joined the acting company in each town and need not have traveled with the troupe).

Mankind could be performed indoors or out, but references in the text suggest that it was originally intended to be performed indoors, in a dining hall—either that of an Inn or that of a public house.[7] When Mankind first welcomes Mercy he says, "All heyl, semely father! Ʒe be welcom to þis house" (209), and when he goes to relieve his bowels Mankind remarks, "I wyll into þi Ʒerde [yard], souerns [soverigns], and cum ageyn son" (561). Later, the rogues decide to play ball, and Newguise shouts to the "hostlere" to lend them a football (732).

The play requires very little in the way of a stage set, and probably none was used in fifteenth-century productions, particularly when the performance was held indoors. Most large dining halls of the time would have had a wall or screen separating them from the kitchen area, with two or sometimes three doors.[8] This screen could form the backdrop for the play, and its doors would serve for some of the entrances and exits. At one point Nought specifically mentions a door, "Go we hens, a deull [devil] wey/ Here ys þe dore, her ys þe wey" (158–59). Much of the play's action is unlocalized, making no specific set demands, but the few actions that could benefit from scenic support, like Mankind's plowing or his attempted suicide by hanging (800–810), could use portable props. When a more elaborate setting is appropriate, the playgoers are asked to imagine it. Mankind goes to pray at church and says simply: "Thys place I assyng [assign] as for my kyrke [church]./ Here in my kerke I knell [kneel] on my kneys" (552–53).

A comfortable informality, almost a cabaret-theatre quality marks the production. Actors enter and exit through the audience (331, 474, 612, 696, 701) and directly address the playgoers who were apparently crowded close to the acting area. Titivillus warns the assembled crowd to keep quiet lest they wake Mankind (589 ff.), and Nought warns Mercy not to dance at the bidding of Newguise and Nowadays, citing the small acting area as his reason: "Trace [dance] not wyth þem, be my cownsell,/ For I haue tracyed sumwhat to fell [too vigorously];/ I tell yt ys a narow space" (95–97). The playgoers are encouraged to join in when the rogues sing their Christmas song, and to help them with the words, Nought (as a modern cabaret singer would do today) cues each line, then Newguise, Nowadays, and all the audience repeat the words in song.

NOUGHT. Now I prey all þe yemandry þat ys here
To synge wyth ws wyth a mery chere:
Yt ys wretyn wyth a coll, yt ys wretyn wyth a cole,
NEW GYSE AND NOWADAYS. Yt ys wretyn wyth a colle, yt is
   wretyn wyth a colle,

(333–36)

An air of informality even extends to the collection of an admission fee from the audience. Just before the apparently spectacular appearance of the Devil, the rogues interrupt the play to go out into the audience to collect money.

NEW GYSE. Now gostly to owr purpos, worschypfull souerence,	[*seriously*]
We intende to gather mony, yf yt plesse yowr neclygence,	
For a man wyth a hede þat ys of grett omnipotens.	[*head*]
NOWADAYS. Kepe yowr tayll, in goodnes I prey yow, goode broþer!	[*tally*]
He ys a worschyppul man, sers, sauying yowr reuerens.	
He louyth no grotys, nor pens of to pens.	[*two-penny pieces*]
Gyf ws rede reyalls yf ȝe wyll se hys abhomynabull presens.	[*red royals*]
New Gyse. Not so! Ȝe þat mow not pay þe ton, pay þe tother.	[*may; the one*]

(459–66)

What else this passage signifies about the mode of performance is of course anybody's guess—perhaps *Mankind* was performed by professional or semiprofessional actors, perhaps amateur actors collect money on behalf of the local monastery or parish church. But this earliest extant reference in an English play to collecting money from the audience does suggest that the playwright and actors must have been fairly confident that their play would be well received, since they wait until the audience has seen almost half of it before asking for their money. And it suggests, too, that the Devil must have been an exciting and popular character in the play, since the audience is assumed willing to pay for the chance to see him onstage.

With the exception of Titivillus's outfit, the costumes and props, like the other elements of the production, were relatively simple. Mercy, who is called a "clerk" by Nowadays (128, 134), "master" by Nought (143), and "father" by both Nought (85) and Mankind (209, 899), was probably dressed as a priest, in cassock and surplice.[9] The text gives no clue about Mischief's costume, but his function as Mercy's foil would make it likely that he too was in clerical garb, perhaps a cassock or religious habit, without a surplice.[10] Mercy addresses him as "brother" (53, 64, 68), and that would be an unlikely form of address if Mischief were costumed as a vice.[11] The other three rogues frequently call him "master" (422, 425, 655, 664, 672), further evidence that he was costumed as someone of socially superior rank. There is less question about the costumes worn by Newguise, Nowadays, and Nought who must have appeared in the most outlandish of new fashions. The three are representatives of all that is worldly and ephemeral and demonstrate this later in the play when they have Mankind's long coat cut down to a short jacket, more stylish than valuable as a defense against the cold (672–721).

Mankind begins the play dressed as a farmer, wearing his long coat (referred to as a "side gown" (671) by Newguise); he carries a spade, a sack of seed corn, rosary beads, paper, and a pen. While still in the state of grace he uses the pen and paper to make a badge for his coat, writing in Latin the words of the ritual blessing with ashes on Ash Wednesday, "Remember man that you are dust, and unto dust you shall return."

Titivillus, the devil with the head "of grett omnipotens" (461), whose presence is said to be "abhomynabull" (465), completes *Mankind*'s cast of two clerics, three fops, and a farmer. The text doesn't elaborate further on Titivillus's appearance, but contemporary representations of the Devil usually show him with horns and a tail. In this play he carries a net that can make him invisible when hung before a victim's eyes, a board which he puts under the ground to hamper Mankind's digging, and a sack full of weeds; he enters with a mocking echo of God's opening line in most of the mystery cycles: "Ego sum dominantium dominus [I am the lord of lords]" (475).

The only other necessary props are a scourge for Mercy, a rope, a gallows tree, a halter, pen and paper for Nought, bandages for Newguise, Nowadays, and Nought, a dish and platter, church goods—possibly candlesticks[12]—a weapon, fetters, and a flute. All of these could easily be carried by a traveling company or borrowed locally.

What kind of audience this traveling troupe expected at their play has been the subject of scholarly controversy, and commentators have contended that the bawdy language and farmer hero prove *Mankind* to have been intended for an audience of farmers and other rustics.[13] The evidence in the text hardly supports this notion but suggests, to the contrary, that the play's fifteenth-century audience included people of various social ranks, like Shakespeare's audience 125 years later. Mercy's opening address to those assembled indicates that the playgoers are of different social ranks: "O ye souerens that sitt, and ye brothern that stonde right uppe" (29). It is to the sovereigns that the play's sophisticated comedy, Latinate puns, and aureate diction must have been addressed, since it's unlikely that the rustics present would have fully appreciated or understood these features. For example, when Nought keeps a written record of the proceedings of Mischief's mock court, he illustrates his own character by writing "Blottibus in blottis/ Blottorum blottibus istis" (680–81)—a record which Mischief reads aloud to the audience and Nowadays punningly calls "a goode rennynge fyst [running, or cursive handwriting]" (683). As the court proceedings continue, Nought writes more fake Latin which is held up for scorn to the audience. Moreover, the many actual Latin words and phrases are neither translated nor paraphrased in an adjacent English line—as they are in *The Castle of Perseverance*—yet the Latin in *Mankind* is often essential to an understanding of the play. An audience composed entirely of rustics would have missed as well much of the humor in Mischief's satirical parody of Mercy's clerical philosophizing (45–63), though they probably would have understood Mischief's complaint that Mercy's manner of speaking is "full of predicacyon" (47) and Mercy's objection that his "talkyng delectable" (65) has been interrupted. And the rustics surely would have agreed with Newguise's assessment that Mercy's body is "full of Englysch Laten" (124). Thus, even when indulging in sophisticated comedy, *Mankind* is never so obscure that the farmers in the audience would lose interest in what is going on, or miss the point altogether. The flamboyant combination of barnyard realism and rhetorical figuration offers something of interest to all social classes, and by including enough to please both rustics and knights, *Mankind* must have been a good commercial enterprise.

Simple in sets and costumes but complex in characterization, language, and style, *Mankind* is fast-moving theatre presenting the standard morality play sequence of innocence/fall/ redemption (here it is more accurately repentance) in less than an hour and a half. The presentation alternates between sections of ornate sermonizing—about twenty-five minutes in all —and sections of concretely realistic plotted action—about fifty-five minutes of the total. The play seems uneven and disorganized primarily because the plot doesn't extend from beginning to end and because on those occasions when the plot does take over from the sermon, the presentation includes much more realistic stage action and individualized, quasi-fictionalized characters than it does in the sections of sermonizing. But the unevenness is more of a problem when we read the play, since in a live performance, the acting techniques, the staging, the style, and the rhythm of the language would highlight the play's organizing form as an illustrated sermon, drawing attention to the fact that the plotted sections are fictionalized illustrations of the concepts presented in the expository sections of sermonizing. Lacking the opportunity to witness such a performance, we can still recognize how the differences complement one another, creating an overall harmony of purpose and design, if we go through the play, focusing on the order and function of its various sections.

In the first forty-four lines of *Mankind*, Mercy delivers an expository sermon on Mankind's fallen nature, giving the audience a number of memorable *sententiae*: "Dyverte not yowrsylffe in tyme of temtacyon" (19); "In goode werkys I awyse yow, souerence, to be perseuerante" (25); "Pryke not yowr felycytes in thyngys transytorye" (30); "The corn xall be sauyde, þe chaffe xall be brente [burnt]" (43). The sermon is then interrupted as Mischief enters, irreverently mocks Mercy, and refutes his biblical proverb about corn and chaff before he finally explains why he has interrupted: "I say, ser, I am cumme hedyr to make yow game" (69). The scene illustrates Mischief's character, but the verbal sparring has little relation to the plot. Next Newguise, Nowadays, and Nought enter, the first two apparently using a rod or switch to make Nought dance wildly.[14] This is the first physical action in the play, and Mercy tries to stop it: "Do wey, do wey þis reull [revel], sers! do wey!" (82). Mercy asks their names and when they tell him he says: "Be Jhesu Cryst þat me dere bowte/ 3e betray many men" (116–17). Mercy and the rogues exchange verbal barbs which neither pre-

sent nor advance the plot, and by the time the rogues exit singing (161), they have established themselves as irreverent fellows, but have done little else. Up to the point where Mankind
finally makes his entrance (185), there has been no dramatic
action other than the interruption of Mercy's sermonizing by
Mischief and the rogues—an interruption that serves as an illustrative vignette of Mercy's warnings.

The initial scene between Mercy and Mankind involves a
discussion about the body/soul dichotomy that Mankind introduces in his opening speech. Mercy tells Mankind, "The
temptacyon of þe flesch ȝe must resyst lyke a man,/ For þer ys
euer a batell betwyx þe soull and þe body" (226–27); "Oppresse
yowr gostly [spiritual] enmy and be Crystys own knyght"
(229); "Yf ȝe wyll be crownyde, ȝe must nedys fyght" (231);
"Mesure ys tresure. Y forbyde yow not þe vse./ Mesure yowrsylf
euer; be ware of excesse./ Þe superfluouse gyse I wyll þat ȝe
refuse" (237–39). Mercy then illustrates the concept of moderation with an example about how a rider should not overfeed
his horse if he wants to rule it and not be thrown into the mud
(241–44). Mercy's earlier example about corn and chaff had
triggered Mischief's initial interruption of the sermon (45 ff.),
and this next descent from the abstract to the particular and
practical is the cue for the rogues to interrupt him once again.
The interruption is short this time and simply serves to further
exemplify the rogues' characterization, providing a concrete
example for Mercy's next major warnings: "Be ware of New
Gyse, Nowadays, and Nought./ Nyse [foolish] in þer aray, in
language þei be large [licentious];/ To perverte yowr condycyons all þe menys [means] xall be sowte" (294–96); "Be ware
of Tytivillus, for he lesyth no wey [misses no chance],/ Þat goth
invysybull and wyll not be sen [seen]./ He wyll ronde [whisper]
in yowr ere and cast a nett befor yowr ey" (300–303).

Mercy finally exits (309), Mankind remarks on the value of
the lessons he has learned and begins to dig in his field, and the

sermonizing that has consumed most of this first third of the play gives way at last to a plotted sequence of actions illustrating Mankind's fight for salvation. Newguise enters from a door in the screen wall, Nowadays and Nought enter through the audience, and the three deride Mankind about his work and try to make him give it up. But Mankind wants no part of them and successfully resists their temptations, bashing them with his spade. He concludes this scene by reminding the audience that he has done exactly what Mercy had advised: "My fadyr Mercy avysyde me to be of a goode chere/ Ande agayn my enmys manly for to fyght" (403–4).

Having won the battle (but not the war), Mankind leaves the stage to fetch seed for his land and the action continues without him. The three rogues complain to Mischief of their beating by Mankind, and in a comic scene reminiscent of the mummers' plays, Mischief says he will heal them by first chopping off the injured part of their body and then putting it back whole again (434–50).[15] The three hastily reassure him they are not that badly injured. The scene has echoes of the springtime season, and adds a faintly pagan and magical aura to the characterization of the rogues; it does little, however, to advance the plot.

After the complete interruption of the play while Newguise, Nowadays, and Nought collect money from the audience, Titivillus appears, sends the rogues off to rob and riot, and begins the job of successfully tempting Mankind. The temptation scene is motivated within the plot by the injuries the rogues have sustained at the point of Mankind's spade—Titivillus is to be their revenge on Mankind. The revenge motive is a flimsy one and yields quickly to the real purpose of this scene as an illustration of Mercy's earlier warnings to Mankind. Titivillus reaffirms what Mercy has said about him: "Euer I go invysybull, yt ys my jett [fashion],/ Ande befor hys ey þus I wyll hange my nett/ To blench [blind] hys syght" (529–31). Totally helpless before Titivillus's magic powers, Mankind reacts instantly to each of his suggestions—responses which seem wholly out of character for someone who so recently had repulsed the three rogues, but which, as we shall see, fit perfectly into the play's artistic design.

To make Mankind abandon his work, Titivillus slips a board under the earth, making it impossible to dig, and laces Mankind's seed with weeds; Mankind tries to dig:

Thys londe ys so harde yt makyth
   wnlusty and yrke.   [*tired and irritated*]
I xall sow my corn at wynter and
   lett Gode werke.   [*at random, without plowing*]
Alasse, my corn ys lost! here ys a
   foull werke!
I se well by tyllynge lytyll xall I wyn.

                                        (545–48)

Mankind throws down his spade and gives up. Next, Mankind begins his "Pater noster" and Titivillus whispers into his ear, "Aryse and avent þe [*relieve yourself*]! nature compellys" (560). Immediately, Mankind says, "I wyll into þi ȝerde, souerens, and cum ageyn son [soon]" (561). Mankind returns and falls asleep, and Titivillus whispers in his ear that Mercy has stolen a mare and been hung in France. He tells Mankind to "Aryse and aske mercy of Neu Gyse, Nowadays, and Nought" (602) and to take a mistress. He then bids farewell to the audience saying, "I haue brought Mankynde to myscheff and to schame" (606). Mankind wakes immediately and says:

Whope who! Mercy hath brokyn hys neke-kycher, avows,
Or he hangyth by þe neke hye wppon þe gallouse.
Adew, fayer masters! I wyll hast me to þe ale-house
Ande speke wyth New Gyse, Nowadays and Nought
And geett me a lemman wyth a smattrynge face.   [*woman; pretty*]
                                        (607–11)

Mankind joins up with the three rogues and twice asks them for mercy (650, 658). These two requests are motivated by the earlier event in the plot when Mankind injured the three with his spade, but more importantly the two statements turn the whole theological order of things upside down and mark the complete reversal of Mankind's spiritual fortunes.

Mankind is now two-thirds complete, and the plot has presented an extended illustration of Mankind first following, then ignoring Mercy's advice. There is little motivation in the plot itself for Mankind's various responses. His rebuff of Newguise, Nowadays, and Nought comes almost immediately after Mercy has delivered his warnings, but there's no implication that Mankind succeeds because that advice is fresh in his mind. Once Titivillus arrives on the scene, poor Mankind gives up his work, prayer, and hope without trying to resist. His fall is not an internally believable response to Titivillus's persuasiveness as a tempter but, rather, seems to be the direct result of the Devil's cleverness as a magician. The real reason Mankind first succeeds and then fails is because the plot exists to demonstrate Mankind's spiritual strengths and weaknesses and to dramatically illustrate Mercy's warnings. It's a dramatization, not a drama.

Mischief now sets up a mock manorial court and Mankind displays his complete commitment to a life of sin by swearing "I wyll, ser" to Mischief's orders that he commit adultery (703–4), rob, steal, and kill (708), go to the alehouse instead of mass and matins (712), and carry a dagger to rob travelers on the highway (714–16). Demonstrably steeped in sin, Mankind ignores Mercy's call to "fle þat felyschyppe" (726) and goes off instead to the alehouse.

Here again, the plot supplies only a weak motivation for Mankind's abrupt willingness to embrace a life of sin. The Devil has suggested that Mankind seek the good will of Newguise, Nowadays, and Nought and told him to take a mistress

(603–4), but there is nothing about robbing, stealing, and kill-
ing, or going to the alehouse in the Devil's temptations. If we
look beyond the plot to Mercy's sermon, the scene becomes
fully motivated. It exists to demonstrate what happens when
Mankind casts in his lot with worldly vanities and to exemplify the inconstancy of Mankind's nature—a subject Mercy
will dwell on in his upcoming exposition, when he says of
Mankind: "I dyscomende and dysalow þin oftyn mutabylyte.
. . . As þe fane [weather vane] þat turnyth wyth þe wynde, so
þou art despectyble" (746–52). Mischief's mock court thus
contrasts with God's holy court, and Mankind, who "ys so
flexybull" (741), is caught in the middle.

Mercy's anger soon turns to sorrow and pity and he prays "O
goode Lady and Moþer of mercy, haue pety and compassyon/
Of þe wrechydnes of Mankynde, þat ys so wanton and so frayll!/
Lett mercy excede justyce, dere Moþer, amytt þis supplyca-
cyon" (756–58). He explains that Newguise, Nowadays, and
Nought have perverted Mankind (762–63), attributing their
success to their alluring ways. Mischief and his three cohorts
once more make fun of Mercy, and their derisive tone contrasts
sharply with Mercy's prayer for forgiveness. Finally, just moments before Mischief and the rogues are about to help Mankind hang himself in despair, Mercy drives off the four enemies
with a scourge and asks Mankind to give him "nethyr golde
nor tresure, but yowr humbyll obeysyance,/ The voluntary syb-
jeccyon of yowr hert" (817–18).

Each event in the plot has illustrated, in roughly the same
order, something Mercy said in his earlier sermon. "Be ware
of New Gyse, Nowadays, and Nought" (294); "Do truly yowr
labure and kepe yowr halyday" (300); "Be ware of Tytivillus . . ." (301); "Yf ȝe dysples [displease] Gode, aske mercy
anon,/ Ellys Myscheff wyll be redy to brace [embrace] yow in
hys brydyll [halter]" (305–6). The sermonizing is the major
motivating force for the actions; they exist to illustrate and

exemplify the ideas in the sermon, and the entire play alternates between exposition and demonstration.

The plot ends when Mankind asks for mercy from God
(834–38) for his fall into sin, and the play closes with Mercy
glossing the allegory, Mankind making additional expository
comments.

> I seyd before, Titiuillus wold asay ȝow a bronte.
> Be ware fro hensforth of hys fablys delusory. . . .
> Ȝe hawe thre aduersaryis and he ys mayster of hem all:
> That ys to sey, the Dewell, þe World, þe Flesch and þe Fell.   [*skin*]
> The New Gyse, Nowadayis, Nowgth, þe World we may hem call;
> And propyrly Titiuillus syngnyfyth the Fend of helle;
>
> The Flesch, þat ys þe vnclene concupissens of ȝour body.
> These be ȝour three gostly enmyis, in whom ȝe hawe put ȝour confidens
> Þei browt ȝow to Myscheffe to conclude ȝour temporall glory,
> As yt hath be schewyd before þis worcheppyll audiens.
>
> (880–90)

The end echoes the beginning; Mercy explains once again
about Mankind's enemies, expositorily restating what the plot
has illustratively presented. Mercy delivers the final three
stanzas to all in the audience, asking them to examine their
spiritual conditions and to remember that this world is vanity.

The major organizing principle in *Mankind* is not plot but,
rather, the expository sermon, illustrated with dramatized examples. In its barest outline, the play first presents its doctrine
conceptually, illustrates a portion of that doctrine with a short
vignette, returns to an expository presentation of doctrine, dramatizes its lessons concretely with entertaining, comic, and
quasi-fictional examples, and ends with an expository gloss of
those examples and a summary of the moral doctrines they
illustrate. The sermonizing and its illustrations intertwine,
since elements in each link the sections together, and the sermon supplies the ultimate motivation for the sequence of il-

lustrative actions presented in the plot. In this respect, *Mankind* differs markedly from plays like *Everyman*, or the Brome *Abraham and Isaac*, where an expository sermon is tacked on at the end of the plot to draw attention to the moral lesson embedded in the preceding story.

Because the play's form is an illustrated sermon, Mischief, Newguise, Nowadays, Nought, and Titivillus can be more fictively drawn, and Mercy and Mankind don't constantly need to maintain their allegorical characterization. Their characterization is motivated from within the play rather than from outside in the realm of moral doctrine. Thus, Mercy is more than simply a presentation of mercy; he is also a preacher, a spiritual guide to Mankind, and a character in the fictional illustration of his own sermon. Hence, he preaches moderation (237 ff.), he is tripped (113), he is angry at Mankind's moral inconstancy (741), he drives off the rogues with a scourge (807), and so forth. Mankind too is both a type character and an individual sinner, a particular man in the dramatization sections of the play.

Mankind presents the standard morality play sequence of innocence/fall/redemption (or repentance) in a totally different form than the one used in *The Castle of Perseverance*. Instead of having a complex, two-part plot extend from beginning to end, *Mankind*'s structure intersperses moral sermonizing with dramatized illustrations of the sermon material (see Figure *10*). Because the sections of moral sermonizing motivate and explain the plotted sections that interrupt them—because these plotted sections exist primarily to illustrate the sections of sermonizing—the plot of *Mankind* has, despite its higher level of vulgar comedy, horseplay, and action-based realism, a more rhetorical structure than the plot of *The Castle of Perseverance*. In fact, the comedy in *Mankind* serves the rhetoric by making the illustrative examples in which it occurs more memorable and effective through parody and contrast.[16]

But in spite of its highly rhetoricized plot, the complexities of *Mankind*'s structure and the precision of its design are capable of affording aesthetic pleasure as well. As we've seen, the same basic pattern is used to arrange each major structural component in *Mankind*, a pattern of alternation between two opposing poles. The points of opposition are different, of course, because the structural components are different, but the arrangement of those components in terms of their individual oppositions is consistent with each. Rhyme and rhythm alternate between the decorous form used by Mercy and Mankind (in grace), and the more colloquial form used by the Devil, the rogues, and Mankind in sin. Mercy and Mankind in grace speak in an elevated, aureate, and abstract diction, whereas the rogues and Mankind in sin use a more realistic, concrete, and natural diction, speaking in more elevated terms only for comic or parodic purposes. These and the other features of style—the rhetorical ornaments, sentence structure, abstract and concrete nouns, conceptual and perceptual adjectives and adverbs, proverbial sayings, and so forth—are distributed

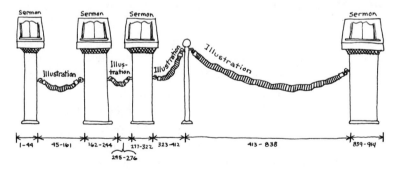

10. Design of *Mankind*. Original drawing by Robert Hickey

throughout the play in such a way that the style shifts back and forth, flamboyantly, between idealized ornate rhetorical figuration and particularized bourgeois realism.

The characters exhibit a similar kind of structural undulation. Mercy is the aloof generalization, alternating between purely allegorical personification and moral adviser, yet never coming across as a fully realized individual. Mischief, Newguise, Nowadays, and Titivillus are presented as quasi-fictional, particularized, even specific individuals. Fittingly, Mankind's language and character alternate in the same way as he interacts first with Mercy, then with the rogues, and finally with Mercy again at the end of the play.

Supported by these other components, the overall structure of meaning in *Mankind* shifts back and forth from exposition to dramatized illustration, from serious sermonizing to grimly comic exemplification. What appears at first to be disorganized and undirected variation is in fact a delicately balanced, harmonious undulation of multiple structures, each participating in the same principle of design.

The undulating form of the play functions to symbolize Mankind's dual nature—the body/soul dichotomy—and we might even argue that the form itself is one side of an intricate and unusual allegorical construct. When he first appears on stage, Mankind explains his dual nature literally: "My name ys Mankynde. I haue my composycyon/ Of a body and of a soull, of condycyon contrarye./ Betwyx þem tweyn ys a grett dyvisyon" (194–96). This duality is symbolized, even allegorized structurally by the play as Mankind first repels Newguise, Nowadays, and Nought, then succumbs to the wiles of Titivillus, but returns to grace again through Mercy's intercession. The duality is further underscored in this pun-filled play by Mercy's two references to the hero as Mankind/ Man Unkind: "Thynke well in yowr hert, yowr name ys Mankynde;/ Be not wnkynde to Gode, I prey yow be hys seruante" (279–80); "I kan not bere yt ewynly þat Mankynde ys so flexybull./ Man onkynde, wheruer þou be!" (741–42). Unquestionably, Mankind's spiritual alternation, his moral flexibility is the central message of the play, a message which the design structurally echoes and figuratively expresses.

Criticisms of the play have either seized on its vulgar comedy or accused it of being a badly conceived moral allegory, since its evil characters don't fit neatly into a clear theological scheme.[17] When we recognize that the comedy serves the instructural purpose by parody and contrast, and that the rogues are basically fictive creations whose purpose is to illustrate the doctrines presented in Mercy's sermons, these difficulties evaporate, and *Mankind* can be appreciated for what it is—a flamboyantly illustrated sermon, displaying a consistency of design that is both rhetorically effective and structurally harmonious.

Chapter 4
Number as Design
Wisdom

The standard morality play sequence of innocence/fall/redemption placed few structural or creative restraints on the fifteenth-century playwrights who used it. In *The Castle of Perseverance* and *Mankind* we have seen two completely different designs for the same basic sequence. The third play in the Macro manuscript, *Wisdom*, presents that sequence in still another pattern, one that can fairly be described as aesthetically masterful, though it is neither a drama nor a dramatization.

The playwright's handling of characterization in *Wisdom* differs markedly from that in the other two Macro plays. The hero is not a single character—Mankind—who typifies all men but is ornately fragmented into allegorical abstractions of various elements of the soul of man, Anima, and her various powers or attributes: Mind, Will, Understanding, and the Five Wits. Yet Anima's chief ally and spiritual adviser is not an allegorical abstraction, or even a guardian angel, but Christ Who is Wisdom; and the chief and only tempter is neither a vice nor a minor demon, but Lucifer, the Prince of Darkness. The reasons for this seeming inconsistency will soon become clear.

The play opens with a theological tutorial as Wisdom teaches Anima about knowing, loving, and serving God, relating these responsibilities to the five wits and three powers of the soul and reminding Anima to avoid her three major enemies: World, Flesh, and Devil. After Wisdom has urged Anima to fight for the crown of glory (307), Lucifer enters, and in a masterful debate with Mind, Will, and Understanding, convinces them that they should abandon the contemplative life and enjoy the world's pleasures. But life in the world quickly leads to sin, and Lucifer stirs Mind to pride, Understanding to covetousness, and Will to lechery.

Steeped in sin, the three Mights demonstrate their fallen status by singing, discussing how they can corrupt the legal system, and dancing. Wisdom reappears and urges the three to repent, but they resist until Wisdom shows them a grossly disfigured Anima. After Wisdom preaches the mercy of God and the Church's requirement for contrition, confession, and due satisfaction, Anima and her Mights and Wits exit, singing a dirge, to be reconciled with the Church. While they are away, Wisdom outlines nine points pleasing to God, and when he is through, Anima (no longer disfigured) reenters with her Mights and Wits, singing a hymn of praise. Anima speaks lovingly of God and ends the play with an exhortation encouraging the audience to follow Wisdom's doctrine and strive for perfection.

Wisdom is essentially an intellectual work, but it is not entirely lacking in the usual flamboyant spectacle. It is enlivened by five songs, three dances, and two processions. When Lucifer has finished tempting the Mights he snatches a mischievous boy from the audience and carries him off. The three Mights quarrel; seven boy devils appear from under Anima's cape when she is in sin, and various characters enter and exit as the play progresses. Except for these isolated events, *Wisdom* presents no physical actions and cannot be said to have a plot.

Though plotless, *Wisdom* is by no means formless. It has relentless, almost mechanical precision and consistency, an intricate structural and rhetorical pattern, that would be impressive enough in a lyric poem but is fairly astonishing in a 1,163-line stage piece. Its style is characteristically flamboyant; augmenting the complex and ornate allegory of the soul and its powers and wits, the playwright makes full use of aureate terms, Latin quotations, rhetorical figures, and symbols to produce a highly decorative display. Wisdom's opening stanzas of self-description are heavily embellished with aureate words and the inverted noun-adjective word order associated with the elegance of French.[1]

Yff ʒe wyll wet þe *propyrte*   [*know*]
Ande þe resun of my *nayme imperyall,*
I am clepyde of hem þat in erthe be [*called by them*]
Euerlastynge Wysdom, to my *nobley* [*equal in value to my nobleness*]
 egalle;
Wyche name acordyt best *in* [*is especially fitting*]
 especyall
And most to me ys convenyent, [*is appropriate*]
Allthow eche persone of þe Trinyte be
 wysdom eternall
And all thre on euerlastynge
 wysdome *togedyr present.*

Neuerþeles, forasmoche as wysdom
 ys propyrly
Applyede to þe Sune by resune,
And also yt fallyt to hym specyally [*is fitting*]
Bycause of hys hye generacyon,

Therfor þe belowyde Sone hathe þis   [*beloved*]
   sygnyficacyon
Custummaly Wysdom, now Gode,   [*according to custom*]
   now man,
Spows of þe chyrche and wery patrone,   [*spouse; protector*]
Wyffe of eche chose sowle. Thus   [*chosen; Thus was the*
   Wysdom begane.   *beginning of Wisdom*]
                          (My italics; 1–16)

The poet sets many of the aureate words in rhyme position, drawing attention to them, further heightening their decorative effect. Here, and in his other speeches, Wisdom favors abstract nouns, static verbs, and conceptual adjectives, all of which provide him with a fittingly aloof and majestic tone.

Anima signals her spiritual kinship to Wisdom by echoing his use of aureate and generally abstract language and inverted word order in her initial conversation with him.

ANIMA. O worthy spowse and
   soueren fayer,   [*fair*]
O swet *amyke,* owr joy, owr blys!   [*beloved*]
To yowr loue wo dothe *repeyer,*   [*whoever doth resort*]
All *felycyte* yn þat *creature ys.*
Wat may I yeue yow ageyn for þis,   [*give; again for this*]
O creator, louer of yowr creature?   [*lover*]
Though be owr freelte we do amys,   [*frailty; wrong*]
Yowr grett mercy euer sparyth
   reddure.   [*rigorous punishment*]

A soueren Wysdom, *sanctus*   [*holy of holies*]
   sanctorum,
Wat may I yeue to yowr most   [*give; most pleasing to you*]
   plesaunce?
WISDOM. *Fili, prebe michi cor tuum.*   [*Son, give me your heart*]
I aske not ellys of all þi *substance.*   [*nothing else; thy substance*]

Thy clene hert, þi meke *obeysance*,   [*obedience*]
Yeue me þat and I am contente.   [*give me that*]
ANIMA. A, soueren joy, and my herty<
  affyance,   [*reliance*]
The *fervowre* of my loue to yow I   [*fervor*]
  present.

(My italics; 69–84)

The terminology is reminiscent of the language of courtly love, and the ornate style suits the matter. The Latin phrases and the repetition of the words "creature" and "creator" in the first stanza, "heart" (in both English and Latin) in the second stanza, and "love" and "give" in both stanzas are a decorative means of signaling the mutual admiration of Wisdom and the soul in grace.

Both Wisdom and Anima make extensive use of this rhetorical figure of repetition in the lengthy opening tutorial and this serves to link their dialogue together. When Anima first enters, she says "I haue louyde [loved] Wysdom as for my lyght,/ For all goodnes wyth hym ys broughte./ In wysdom I was made all bewty bryghte" (22–24). Wisdom says in his next speech, "I am foundon lyghte wythowt comparyson,/ Off sterrys aboue all þe dysposicyon,/ Forsothe of lyght þe very brightnes" (28–30).

A little further on, Anima says: "A, soueren Wysdom, yff [if] yowur benygnyte/ Wolde speke of loue, þat wer [would be] a game [delightful]" (39–40); Wisdom responds: "Off my loue to speke, yt ys myrable [wonderful]./ Beholde now, Sowll, wyth joyfull mynde,/ How louely [lovely] I am, how amyable,/ To be halsyde [embraced] and kyssyde of mankynde" (41–44).

"Love" is repeated frequently in this section. Wisdom says, "What wrech is that louyth [loveth] not this loue/ Þat louyt [loves] hys louers euer [ever] so tendyrly" (66–67), and Anima takes up the word in her response quoted above (69–84). A little further on, "knowing" is repeated.

ANIMA. O endles Wysdom, how may I haue   [*have*]
  knowynge
Off þi Godhede incomprehensyble?
WISDOM. By knowynge of yowrsylff ȝe may haue
  felynge   [*feeling*]
Wat Gode ys in yowr sowle sensyble.
The more knowynge of yowr selff passyble,   [*sensitive self*]
Þe more veryly ȝe xall God knowe.   [*truly you shall*]
                                         (93–98).

This opening section with Wisdom and Anima together extends for 164 lines before the Five Wits and the three Mights —Mind, Will, and Understanding—enter. Key concepts emphasized here through repetition include "wisdom," "creature," "give," "heart," "love," "know," "sin," and "light"; they climax with Wisdom's description of the uses of reason and his summary of man's primary responsibility to his Creator.

The other parte, þat ys clepyde   [*called reason*]
  resone,
Ande þat ys þe ymage of Gode   [*image of God particularly*]
  propyrly,
For by þat þe sowll of Gode hathe   [*that; the soul has knowledge
  cognycyon   of God*]
And be þat hym serwyt and louevyt   [*by that; loves and serves him*]
  duly

                                       (141–44)

These ideas are basic tenets of medieval theology: because he has reason, man is made in the image of God and must do all in his power to know, love, and serve Him according to the commandment.[2]

Aureate diction and other rhetorical figures, including metaphor and (not surprisingly) repetition, also decorate the introductory speeches of the Mights in grace. In addition to the repetition of individual words, Mind repeats a series of syntactically similar phrases in his opening stanza: "How holl [whole] I was mayde, how fayere [fair], how fre [free],/ How gloryus, how jentyll [noble] to hys lyknes [likeness]" (187–88). Will repeats the same word in different senses, punning on his name.

Wyth goode wyll no man may spyll   [*may be damned*]
Nor wythowt goode wyll of blys be   [*bliss*]
  sure.
Wat soule wyll gret mede recur,   [*great wealth obtain*]
He must grett wyll haue, in thought
  or dede   [*deed*]

                                                         (215–18)

Owr wyll in Gode must be only sett   [*placed*]
And for Gode to do wylfully.
Wan gode wyll resythe, Gode ys in   [*When good will rises*]
  ws knett   [*drawn*]
Ande he performyt þe dede veryly.   [*deed truly*]

                                                         (229–32)

Ornamental stanza form provides another decoration. Wisdom, Anima, and the three Mights in grace generally use eight-line stanzas, often divided between two speakers and rhyming *a b a b b c b c*. This more stately ballad stanza contrasts with the *rime couée* stanzas spoken by Lucifer and the three Mights in sin, which rhyme *a a a b a a a b*. When Wisdom reappears and calls on the sinful Mights to repent (873 ff.), they appropriately respond to him in the ballad stanza, *a b a b b c b c*, reverting to this more dignified form in deference to Wisdom's rank and importance. Unlike the speeches of demons in the other moralities, Lucifer's stanzas in this play are heavy with aureate diction, since like Wisdom, Lucifer is a clever rhetorician, and although the rhythm of his stanzas is less dignified, his embellished diction indicates that he is a suitably matched opponent for Wisdom.

There is just enough perceptual realism in *Wisdom* to establish the second side of the flamboyant duality, but much of it involves the richly detailed costumes, and we can't fully appreciate it without seeing or imagining the play performed. Stage directions indicate that Wisdom dresses in rich purple cloth of gold, with a mantle of the same material lined in ermine. He wears a royal hood trimmed in ermine, a wig fitted with artificial eyebrows, a curly cloth of gold beard, and a rich imperial crown set with precious stones and pearls; he carries a gold ball with a cross on top in his left hand and a scepter in his right hand. To visually link her with Wisdom, Anima is given a similar wig. She dresses as a maid in white cloth of gold handsomely trimmed in miniver, but a black mantle over her white gown reminds the audience that her soul has two aspects—one foul, the other fair—sensuality and reason (149–56). She wears an elaborate headdress laced behind that has two knots of gold hanging down and tassels at the sides. When the Five Wits first appear they too are dressed in white and wear wigs and hats (164). Likewise, Mind, Will, and Understanding dress in white cloth of gold and wear wigs and hats "in sute," though it's not clear from the context whether their wigs are like those of Wisdom and Anima or whether this means only that each of the three Mights wears the same kind of wig.

When they've fallen into sin, the three Mights signal their new spiritual condition by speaking in a more realistic, conversational style. Will says proverbially, "Ya, I woll [will] no more row ageyn [against] þe floode" (491). In response to Lucifer's advice that the three submit to sin and always be merry, Mind answers, "Ya, ellys I beschrew [curse] my snowte!" (506); Understanding says, "And yff I care, cache [catch] I þe gowte!" (507); and Will vows, "And yff I spare, þe Dewyll me spede!" (508). They also change costume, dressing up as gallants in the latest fashions. Mind says, "Lo, me here in a new aray!/ Wyppe, wyrre, care awey!/ Farwell perfeccyon" (552–54). Understanding echoes the same idea: "Ande haue here one as fresche as yow!" (558), and Will says, "Lo, here on [one] as jolye as ʒe!" (566).

The scene with the three Mights in sin presents a fairly realistic catalogue of abuses apparently widespread in the fifteenth-century law courts. But then the two sides of the flamboyant duality are curiously blended as these abuses are allegorized by elaborately costumed retainers who enter and join each of the three Mights in a dance. Mind's followers all dress alike; each has a crest with rampant lions on it, each sports a red beard, and each carries a staff. Mind's primary sin is Pride, illustrated here as Maintenance (the support of false causes), and he introduces his six retainers as they join him on stage: Indignation, Sturdiness (stubbornness), Malice, Hastiness (rash anger), Wretch (revenge), and Discord. Together with Mind they illustrate seven aspects of three sins, Pride, Envy, and Anger (716). They dance together to the music of trumpets, traditionally associated with pomp and thus linked to pride. Understanding's followers are costumed as jurors in gowns with hoods around their necks; they wear hats and masks with two faces to signify their hypocrisy. Understanding's primary sin is Covetousness, presented here in the aspect of perjury. This particular vice, accompanied by his six retainers, Wrong, Sleight, Doubleness, Falseness, Robbery, and Deceit, demonstrate the means to indulge Covetousness. They dance to a minstrel with a bagpipe, often associated with lechery, but here probably emblematic of the covetous man's bursting purse. Will, whose sin is Lechery, is accompanied by six women (three inexplicably disguised as gallants), all masked alike: Recklessness, Idleness, Surfeit and Greediness (apparently represented by one dancer), Adultery, Mistress, and Fornication. Symbolically, their minstrel plays a hornpipe. Whereas Recklessness and Idleness are frequently linked with love (particularly courtly love), they are also aspects of Sloth. Surfeit and Greediness are clearly attributes of Gluttony, and all seven of the deadly sins are thus represented in this series of elaborate dances.[3]

Other elements adding concrete immediacy to *Wisdom* include the theatrical performance itself, with its dances, songs, and processions, and the concrete perceptual images lightly sprinkled through various characters' speeches. Mind says that when he thinks of the years and days of his sinfulness, he knits his brows in sorrow (196). Will speaks of opening "The lybrary of reson" (227). Understanding says that to follow Jesus' law "Ys swetter [sweeter] to me þan sawowre [savor] of þe rose" (338).

The *Wisdom* poet was far less interested in adding vividly realistic touches to his play than either of the other two Macro playwrights, and took pains to assure that the realistic elements he did employ had an accompanying symbolic function. The visually perceptual costumes and dances as well as the more conversational language of the Mights in sin all have a symbolic purpose in the performance, outwardly signaling some abstract, spiritual reality. An interesting example of this combination of realism and symbolism is the play's use of costuming to turn Mind, Will, and Understanding back to a life of grace. When Wisdom first calls on them to repent, the three protest that they are still too young (890). Wisdom then says, "Se howe ye haue dysvyguryde [disfigured] yowr soule!" (901), and stage directions state: "Here ANIMA apperythe in þe most horrybull wyse, fowlere þan a fende" (after 902). She is wearing a "horrible" mantle and seven boy devils come out from under it, run around, and then return. The directions don't specify what makes the mantle horrible or how it could accommodate seven little boys, but we can be sure that the visual effect must have been impressive, since the Mights immediately vow to return to God and begin anew in a life of grace.

Anima weeps for sorrow because of her sin, and the directions indicate that the demons retreat (after 978). But Anima still wears her foul costume and must leave the stage to change both clothes and spirit. When they return sixty-eight lines later, Anima, her Five Wits, and Mind, Will, and Understanding are costumed as they were at the beginning of the play, but now they also wear crowns (after 1064) to symbolize their spiritual victory over sin. The flamboyant blend of symbolism and realistic imagery provides a spectacle for the eyes as well as a visual reinforcement of the play's message. Despite their theatrical impact, however, the costumes and other realistic devices with symbolic overtones are all basically static and give *Wisdom* the distinct flavor of a masque or *tableau vivant*.

Whatever its concrete immediacy, *Wisdom* is, as we've said, an essentially intellectual work. This may well be in part a result of its composition for a very special audience—an audience of clerics. Of the three Macro plays, *Wisdom* seems least suited for performance before a paying audience of laymen and women, and it's unlikely that the play was ever intended for secular performance. *Mankind* and *The Castle of Perseverance* show man how he should ask for mercy and forgiveness when through his human weakness he falls into sin, but *Wisdom* takes an at once more positive and more subtle approach, urging—as one might fittingly urge upon clerics—the continued pursuit of perfection.[4] When Lucifer tempts Mind, Will, and Understanding, he doesn't present his temptation directly but only as an argument for the mixed rather than the contemplative life (405 ff.). Lucifer urges the Mights to "Go in þe worlde, se þat abowte [see what it's all about]" (501)—a temptation that would have little relevance for a lay audience.

Scholarly arguments exist on both sides of the question, with contentions that *Wisdom* was written for monks, laymen, and even possibly law students at the Inns of Court,[5] but the likelihood is that *Wisdom* was written for monks by a monk. The play presents a sophisticated and theologically precise allegory and deals with the subtleties of moral psychology more carefully and in far more detail than an audience of laymen would be likely to appreciate or understand. In its expository form, its lyricism, and its extensive use of song, processional, and dance, the work is reminiscent of eleventh- and twelfth-century Latin ecclesiastical plays. Perhaps equally telling is the absence of references to excretion and sex that abound in *Mankind* and are found to a lesser extent in *The Castle of Perseverance*. Possibly *Wisdom* was performed by novices and juniors for other members of a monastic community—perhaps including the boys in the monastery school, since Lucifer grabs a small boy out of the audience when he leaves (s.d. after 550). The Benedictine Abbey of Bury St. Edmunds, where the manuscript was probably written, would have been one of the few monastic houses in Britain large enough in the fifteenth century to supply the cast of thirty-six which a full performance of the play, including dances, would seem to require. (Smaller communities could perhaps have performed the play with role-doubling and some cutting).[6]

In genre, *Wisdom* might be classified as a paraliturgical masque; its rhetoric is well suited to an audience of monks, and its tone and solemn spectacle would have been theatrically effective with an audience daily exposed to the dramatic beauty of the monastic liturgy.[7] The play has an unlocalized setting, requiring no scenery or stage devices of any kind, and could be performed in a monastery refectory or a chapter house on a raised platform or flat space. It might even have been performed in the abbey church, perhaps in the center aisle between the two choir stalls.

Wisdom is the only play in the Macro manuscript to survive in more than one copy. An incomplete text of the play, comprising the first 752 lines, is included in the famous Digby MS 133, now in the Bodleian Library at Oxford. The Digby text includes five lines and a stage direction not in the Macro text, suggesting that at one time a third manuscript of the play must have existed, since neither of the two texts we have could have been copied from the other. The Digby manuscript was owned by Miles Blomefylde who was born at Bury St. Edmunds in 1525 and signed his name or initials at three different places in the manuscript.[8]

The existence of two copies of the play and the evidence from these that at least one other copy existed in the fifteenth century indicate that *Wisdom* was held in some esteem. Book production at the time was an expensive and tedious process, and a work would not have been copied unless people thought it had some literary, monetary, or spiritual value. As we'll see, the literary merit of *Wisdom* is as impressive as its theological learning. Though it may seem dull fare to twentieth-century tastes, it has the structural consistency and balance of a carefully designed machine—a metaphor I apply to a work of literature with some reluctance, but one surprisingly well suited to this play, since, of the three Macro plays, *Wisdom* appears to have the most schematically thorough organizing principle, a design more mathematical than strictly literary.

Wisdom presents the three-part morality sequence of innocence/fall/redemption in a structure dominated by the number three—a number that has a special perfection as the first ordinal to have a beginning, middle, and end.[9] Most structural elements in the play are organized either in threes or in multiples of three, and the resulting form displays a remarkable mathematical harmony. Those structures not organized by the number three or its multiples draw special attention to themselves because they depart from the scheme, and thus the mathematical design functions as a symbol in itself, reinforcing the perfection or imperfection of the ideas it arranges.

We can begin our survey of *Wisdom*'s mathematical design almost anywhere. Perhaps the most curious evidence of the playwright's fascination with the number three is his disposition of roles and speaking parts. There are thirty-six characters in *Wisdom*, not counting the three minstrels who play three different instruments. Of these thirty-six roles, six characters have speaking parts and the rest are silent participants in dances, processions, or tableaux. The figure of Mankind is allegorically presented in nine aspects: Anima, or the soul of man, Five Wits (who do not speak), and Mind, Will, and Understanding. Lucifer's temptations are directed at these last three, who with their eighteen retainers illustrate the soul in sin.

Wisdom, as Christ, is the second person of the Trinity but he points out in his opening stanza that he embodies all three persons of the Trinity (7–8). Wisdom explains that as the Son of God, he is by custom 1) both God and man, 2) the spouse of the Church, 3) the wife of each chosen soul (15–16).

In their opening tutorial together, Anima makes nine requests for information: 1) Speak of love (40)? 2) What can I give in return for your love (73–74)? 3) What can I give you that will be most pleasurable (78)? 4) Teach me the schools of your divinity (86). 5) How can I have knowledge of your Godhead (93–94)? 6) What is a soul (102)? 7) Why do we carry the sin of the first man (107–8)? 8) How does grace begin anew (119–20)? 9) What things provide the soul with knowledge (133–34)?

Wisdom responds to each in turn and afterward explains that the soul is comprised of two parts. One part is sensuality, served by five wits (a total of six elements, counting sensuality), the other part is reason which consists of three parts: 1) speculative knowledge, 2) practical knowledge, 3) and the ability to love and serve God (135–48). The two sides of man are thus presented in nine aspects: sensuality and the five wits, the speculative reason, the practical reason, and the rational appetite. These last three appear as the characters Mind, Understanding, and Will (which as the rational appetite is subtly distinguished from the concept of free will). It is mankind's two-part nature (and two is a less perfect number than three) which predisposes the soul to sin.

Thus a sowle ys bothe fowlle and fayer: [*is both foul and fair*]
Fowll as a best be felynge of synne,   [*beast; by the experience*]
Fayer as a Angell, of hewyn þe ayer,   [*the heir of heaven*]
By knowynge of Gode by hys reson
   wythin.

(157–60)

The characters in *Wisdom* illustrate the moral allegory, which also is elaborately and painstakingly built upon the number three. After Mind, Will, and Understanding have entered and identified themselves, Wisdom explains their significance first in terms of the Trinity, then in terms of the cardinal virtues, faith, hope, and charity.

Lo, thes thre myghtys in on Soule be: [*one*]
Mynde, Wyll, and Wyndyrstondynge.
By Mynde of Gode þe Fadyr knowyng haue
   ye;
By Wndyrstondynge of Gode þe Sone ye
   haue knowynge;
By Wyll, wyche turnyt into loue   [*into burning love*]
   brennynge,
Gode þe Holy Gost, þat clepyde ys lowe: [*that is called love*]
Not thre Godys but on Gode in beynge.   [*one*]
Thus eche clene soule ys symylytude of   [*each clean*]
   Gode abowe.

By Mynde feythe in þe Father haue we,   [*faith*]
Hoppe in owr Lorde Jhesu by   [*Hope*]
  Wndyrstondynge,
Ande be Wyll in þe Holy Gost charyte: [*charity*]
Lo, thes thre pryncypall wertus of yow   [*virtues spring from you*]
  thre sprynge.
Thys þe clene soule stondyth as a kynge;   [*Thus the clean soul*]
Ande abowe all þis ȝe haue free wyll;   [*you have*]
                                    (277–90)

Wisdom next details the soul's three enemies—World, Flesh, and Devil (294)—and explains how the soul should avoid temptation. Again, the presentation is made in terms of three.

Wan suggestyon to þe Mynde doth apere,   [*appear*]
Wndyrstondynge, delyght not ȝe þerin;   [*delight not you therein*]
Consent not, wyll, yll lessons to lere,   [*evil lessons to learn*]
Ande than suche steryngys be no syn.   [*such stirrings*]
                                    (301–4)

The instructional allegory ends when Anima delivers an elaborately ornate and stylized lyric of praise to the Lord that consists of a long series of subordinate clauses beginning with "when" and ending with a statement of praise introduced by "wherefore." This litany, cast in the format of a legal citation, includes eleven "when" clauses, and one "wherefore" conclusion, producing an echoic repetition twelve times (309–24). After the litany, the Five Wits sing "Tota pulchra es [You are beautiful]"—the Trinity Sunday processional antiphon—and lead a ten-member procession offstage, a procession that includes Anima, Wisdom, Mind, Will, and Understanding. The symbolism of this ten-member procession—breaking the scheme of threes—would not have been lost on the cleverest members of the medieval audience, those who recognized the traditional significance of the number ten, representing the wholeness of the numerical system—the arithmetical limit of the universe—a completeness derived from the sum of the four basic numbers: $1 + 2 + 3 + 4$.[10]

Though the manuscript does not divide the play into separate scenes, there are natural divisions in the play, and this procession marks one of them. When the song has ended, Lucifer enters and begins what might be called the next movement of the play—the temptation and fall of the Mights. Lucifer reiterates Wisdom's explanation about the tripartite soul and says he will tempt the flesh of man because it is so changeable (360). His temptations directly follow Wisdom's earlier outline (301–4).

To þe Mynde of þe Soule I xall mak *suggestyun,*   [*shall make*]
Ande brynge hys Wndyrstondynge to *dylectacyon,*
So þat hys Wyll make *confyrmacyon;*

(My italics; 365–67)

Lucifer exits, changes into the costume of a gallant, and returns to engage the Mights in debate. Following the order he has just outlined, Lucifer tempts in a three-part series. He makes suggestion to Mind that there is a time and place for everything and that when *prayer, fasting,* and *labor* are not done in their proper time, they are done amiss (400–404). He asks rhetorically if it's lawful for a man with a family to leave his work and responsibilities to spend all his time in prayer. He then argues that the mixed life is preferable to the contemplative life, since the contemplative life is a hard one that requires a person to *fast, wake,* and *pray, keep silence, weep,* and *avoid excess* (433, 435), and failure is a great displeasure to God. Mind says, "Truly, me seme [it seems to me] ȝe haue reson" (444).

Lucifer next speaks with Understanding, tempting him to the riches of the world. Understanding responds, "In thys I fele [feel] in manere of dylectacyon" (462), and Lucifer then begins to work on Will. He asks what sin there is in *meat, ale,* and *wine* (473) and urges Will to give up chastity and take a wife. Will responds that "As þe fyue [five] wyttys gyff informacyon,/ Yt semyth yowr resons be goode" (479–80). The three Mights succumb to Lucifer's sophism and demonstrate their fall from grace in statements which again repeat Wisdom's original three-part outline.

MIND. To þis *suggestyon* agre we.   [*agree*]
WNDYRSTONDYNGE. *Delyght* þerin I haue truly.
WYLL. And I *consent* þerto frelye.   [*freely*]
(My italics; 497–99)

Having made their decision to go out into the world, the Mights temporarily exit, and in their absence Lucifer explains to the audience how he will next stir the Mights to *pride, covetousness,* and *lechery* (527), thus assuring the death of the soul. These three major sins are manifestations of the desires which St. John warns against:[11] pride of life, concupiscence of the eyes (covetousness), and concupiscence of the flesh (lechery). These desires are also the antitheses of the three major vows taken by members of religious orders: obedience, poverty, and chastity. Lucifer explains to the audience how these sins will eventually lead to the total destruction of the soul through despair (542), and when he has finished outlining his plan, he grabs a noisy boy from the audience and exits, never to be seen again in the play.

We next observe the Mights in sin, verbally describing various aspects of their respective transgressions. Each comments on his new clothes as he enters, and in the course of their initial banter, Mind bids farewell to perfection, Understanding says good-bye to conscience and truth, and Will takes his leave of chastity (552–69).

The contrast established here between the Mights in sin and their previous life in grace is particularly interesting. Wisdom earlier had likened Mind to God the Father, Understanding to God the Son, and Will to God the Holy Ghost. Each Might now sins directly against that member of the Trinity to which he has been compared. Mind's sin is pride, the father of all sins, and the same sin that Lucifer committed when he opposed God the Father. Understanding sins in covetousness, the unwise use of worldly goods and a direct affront to Wisdom the Son who had said earlier, "Wysdom ys better þan all worldly precyosness" (33). By bidding farewell to Truth, Understanding doubly rejects Wisdom. Finally, Will, who has been linked to the Holy Spirit, abandons the love of God for the love of the flesh by sinning in lechery.[12]

The Mights then describe various aspects of their respective sins. First, Mind-as-pride says that *nature, fortune,* and *grace* (in the debased sense of intellectual cleverness) are of primary solace to him (574–75) and explains the relationship of these three to pride. Then Understanding-as-covetousness says that his special joy is in hoarding wealth. He gives a three-part list of covetous activities, saying he loves to *see wealth, touch it,* and *count it* (583). Will then provides a three-part outline of lechery, saying his greatest joy is in *the latest fashions* (to appear loveable), in *speaking delectable words of love,* and in *hugging and kissing* (589–95). The Mights then sing in harmony, with Mind singing the tenor, Understanding the middle part, and Will the treble.

After the song, the Mights list the ramifications of their individual sins in society at large and the law courts in particular, then each dances with retainers who allegorically present these sins. Six dancers join each Might and each of the three dances thus involves a total of seven characters, which Mind observes "ys a numbyr of dyscorde and inperfyghtnes" (697). Together the three Mights and their companions present twenty-one aspects of the seven deadly sins—a mathematically symbolic means by which the earlier perfection of the number three can be transformed into the imperfection of the number seven.

Will's dance is interrupted by a comic fight, but in a few moments the Mights reconcile and continue discussing ways to increase their wealth. Understanding and Mind each mention three means they will use to enrich themselves at the courts (791, 796), but Will says only that he sometimes snatches the purses of those who have done him no harm. By breaking the three-part symmetry and by apparently being interested more in lovemaking than money, Will further symbolizes the imperfection, the disharmony of the Mights in sin.

The final illustration of their sinfulness comes in a discussion about buying supper. Mind says he will pay one noble (6s.8d.); Understanding at first agrees to pay two nobles (13s.4d.); and Will says he will pay three nobles (£1). When Mind says they should all pay the same, Understanding balks and refuses to pay more than "schylyngys nyne" (830), further demonstrating his covetous character. A brief discussion follows about how they can use the courts to rid Will's cousin Janet of her churlish husband so Will can play lustily with her, and Will ends the sequence in sin saying, "Mery, mery, all mery þan [then] be we!/ Who þat ws tarythe [restrains us], curs [curse] haue he and myn!" (871–72).

At this point the third and final movement of the play begins, as Wisdom reenters and calls on Mind to remember who he is (873). At first all three Mights resist, but when they see Anima's horrible attire and the seven boy devils who accompany her (numerically symbolizing both the seven deadly sins

and the imperfection of the soul in its state of sin), they are
ready to repent. Wisdom asks why the Mights reject his love
and with this the three verbally turn away from sin. Mind says:
"A, lorde! now I brynge to mynde/ My horryble synnys and
myn offens" (925–26); Understanding responds, "Be [by] yow,
Mynde, I haue very knowenge/ That grettly Gode we haue of-
fendyde" (933–34); and Will says, "I wyll retorne to Gode and
new begynne/ Ande in hym gronde [establish] my wyll stable"
(943–44).

Having gotten themselves into sin in threes, they now extri-
cate themselves in threes. Wisdom explains that for full restoration Understanding must have contrition, Mind must make
confession, and Will must do satisfaction (973–75). Anima
weeps for sorrow and the seven devils leave her.[13] But Anima
must still seek mercy from God, and she goes offstage with the
Mights to make confession. While she is away, Wisdom delivers a sermon to the audience on the nine points pleasing to
God: 1) give a penny to the poor; 2) weep one tear for Christ's
passion; 3) suffer a word of reproof from your neighbor pa-
tiently for love of God; 4) wake one hour for love of God;
5) have pity on your sick and needy neighbor; 6) restrain your
speech for God's reverence; 7) do not tempt your neighbor to
evil; 8) pray often; 9) love God sovereignly (997–1064). These
nine are spiritual remedies for the twenty-one aspects of the
Mights in sin because when a man follows these carefully, he
can't commit any of the seven deadly sins.[14]

When Anima reenters, preceded by the Five Wits, flanked by
Mind and Understanding, followed by Will, they are all dressed
as they were at the beginning of the play—a visual contrast to
their costumes when in sin—and they are singing Psalm 115,
verses twelve and thirteen—an aural contrast to the dirge
Anima sang "in þe most lamentabull wyse, wyth drawte [drawn
out] notys [notes]" (s.d. after 996) when she left earlier to seek
mercy.

At the end of this triumphant procession, Anima praises the mercy of God and reviews how she has sinned, summarizing the play's allegory.

In tweyn myghtys of my soule I the offendyde:	[*two; I offended thee*]
The on by my inwarde wyttys, thow ben gostly;	[*one; those are spiritual*]
Þe other by my outwarde wyttys comprehendyde,	
Tho be þe fyve wyttys bodyly;	[*those are*]
Wyth þe wyche tweyn myghtys mercy I crye.	[*with the same two*]
	(1073–77)

The mathematical precision of this explanation of the allegory is quite intricate. Anima has sinned in her powers of sensuality and reason—body and soul. This duality which makes her spiritually frail is one of the things Wisdom warned her about at the beginning of the play (135–60). This two-part, flawed yet unified soul says she has sinned with her inward spiritual wits—Mind, Will, and Understanding—and her outward, or bodily Five Wits. Thus, *Wisdom* presents the human spiritual condition as a nine-part composite—Anima, her Three Mights, and Five Wits—and when Anima admits her sins and asks for mercy, she realigns all nine with the Trinity. Anima's references to the "tweyn [two] myghtys" (1073, 1077) might be confusing for the reader, but in performance, her black and white costume would remind the audience that these are attributes of Anima, aspects allegorized as the Three Mights and Five Wits.

Anima continues her praise of mercy, saying that without it she would be unable to make amends for her trespasses (1080). In this and her frequent other references to mercy in this section, she echoes a central theme of all the moralities. Wisdom notes that although Anima's Five Wits have offended, Christ's five wits which never did offend God have made up for her transgressions through the suffering of the passion. Wisdom goes on to explain that the soul, first reformed by baptism (1109), is now reformed by the sacrament of penance (1111) and has received the crowns of victory (1115)—another series of three elements. Mind, Understanding, and Will then each give, in turn, a one-stanza affirmation of his intention to avoid sin in the future, and Anima ends the play with three stanzas of praise to Wisdom whom *heaven, earth,* and *every creature* should revere (my italics; 1145).

Although the play is divided into four scenes in modern editions (not always the same four), a closer reading reveals a three-part structure, directly paralleling the three-part sequence of innocence (1–324), fall (325–872), and redemption or repentance (873–1163). The rhyme pattern supports and signals this three-part division. In the first and third parts, the stanzas use three rhymes, but in the middle section with the Mights in sin, the stanza form changes to a less mathematically perfect two-rhyme scheme.

The overall three-part structure of *Wisdom* is further segmented into six major movements and three minor or submovements. In a normal play, we would call these "events," "actions," or "incidents." They aren't really any of these, however, since *Wisdom* is basically plotless and is more expository than mimetic, more static than dynamic. The first movement involves the tutorial between Wisdom and Anima. The second movement presents the sophistic argument Lucifer uses to tempt the Mights to sin. Movement three, with its three subparts, displays the Mights in sin, through a) exposition, b) dance, c) conclusion. The fourth movement presents Wisdom's call for repentance and includes the vision of Anima disfigured by sin. Movement five is the sermon on the nine points pleasing to God. Finally, the sixth movement shows Anima restored to grace and the resolve of Anima, her Five Wits, and three Mights to remain in their reformed state.

Everything presented in movements two through six is logically prepared for and foreshadowed in movement one and functions as an extended explanation and demonstration of the ideas presented initially in that tutorial. The play proceeds

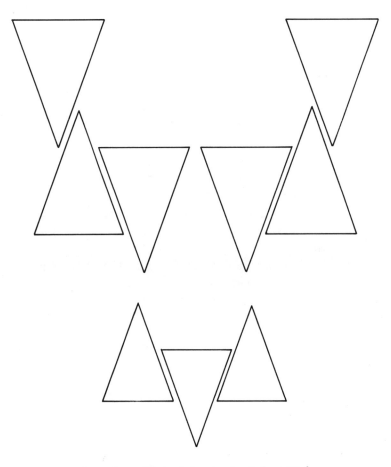

11. Design of *Wisdom*. Original drawing by Robert Hickey

logically and serially, presenting the steady progression of the Mights into and then out of sin. The dances are at the center of the progression—the very depth of the soul's life in sin—flanked on each side by three main movements, and one submovement. (see Figure *11*).

The mathematical symmetry of *Wisdom*, its consistent use of threes or multiples of three to present the three-part fall of man's soul from the life of grace and its three-part return to God's favor, is the secret of its aesthetic brilliance. Rhymes, characters, processions, dances, songs, sermons, temptations, and dramatic movements—all the major structural components—are arranged in terms of threes or multiples of three. These in turn support and present the allegory which is keyed throughout to the Christian concept of a triune God and the parallel idea that man's tripartite soul is made in the image of that God. Here more than in either of the other two Macro plays, form and meaning reinforce one another, design echoes symbol, and symbol is imbedded in design. The whole is marvelously lyrical, a tightly structured presentation of intricate theological dogma in the stately, balanced form reminiscent of the masque.

Although *Wisdom* may fail as drama in the usual sense, it clearly succeeds as a flamboyant celebration.

Chapter 5
Art as Design

If one thing stands out clearly from our analysis of the three Macro plays it is that each has more to offer than a moral message. The plays combine music, song, poetry, costumes, props, and stage action to create entertaining theatrical spectacles. What's more, each play has a distinctly different principle of organization that is pervasive, complex, and aesthetically pleasing. Yet, all three plays are admittedly minor works. We make a distinction, after all, between good art and great art. The greatness of a work of art depends less on how well the piece is made than on how successfully a well-made work—or, if we consider *Moby Dick* or *War and Peace*, even a relatively well-made work—can maintain its appeal from one generation to the next. To put it another way, the beauty of a work of art —what makes it good art—is largely a structural or formal matter, a function of how well each part relates to the others.[1] To be great, however, a good work must also say something substantial; it must be, in a word, *massive*; and it must say what it says in a rhetorically moving way. We usually consider a work to be great if its message has universal human appeal and its structure presents that universally appealing message powerfully. Each of the Macro plays has a grand design and each is lyrically and theatrically impressive, but each falls short of greatness precisely because its characters are presentational rather than representational, the actions they perform are schematic rather than exploratory, or as Aristotle would say, *energeiic*, and their message is narrowly doctrinal rather than humanly universal.

The plays were created as celebration pieces, extravagant reaffirmations of belief in one part of the total Christian message. Allegorically framed, schematized reminders of the nature of sin and its remedies, the need for the sacrament of penance, and the ever-present availability of God's mercy were undoubtedly fascinating and reassuring to an audience that shared a common interest in these subjects and a common belief in the efficacy of Roman Catholicism's specific means for attaining salvation. Other audiences at other times haven't felt strongly enough about these particular doctrines to be deeply moved by an ornate theatrical celebration of them. In short, the Macro plays only marginally survive the test of time because they are too much a part of their own time. They fail as great art because they succeed too well as fifteenth-century religious celebrations.

But the Macro plays remain a rewarding and important subject of study. In addition to their obvious entertainment value (and it is considerable, particularly for those of us who enjoy quaint but well-structured oddities as a relief from modern oddities which offer nothing worth serious contemplation), the plays are especially interesting because they are so much a part of their time—a time of artistic extremism when writers greatly admired and, by exaggeration, tried to emulate the artistry of earlier writers like Chaucer, Langland, the Pearl Poet, and Gower. Writing in late medieval English flamboyant style, the Macro plays' authors exaggerate the features from earlier works that they considered artistically significant, thus highlighting them and giving us the opportunity to observe the ways those elements function artistically.

Though *The Castle of Perseverance, Mankind*, and *Wisdom* survive as a related group only because they were felicitously bound together in a single manuscript volume, they have—despite their individual differences—generic, stylistic, and structural similarities. All three areas of similarity have already been outlined, but because the similarities in structure suggest things about the aesthetic principles of these and other medieval literary works, they perhaps warrant further exploration.

Each of the three plays is alike in mixing some or all of the following contrasting extremes: allegory and realism, moral theology and comedy, rhetorical ornamentation and conversational naturalism, lyrical exposition and physical action, bawdy irreverence and sermonic eloquence, stately ceremony and topical satire. This mixture of dissimilar components is by no means unique to the Macro plays. Historians and art critics have long recognized the combination of apparently unrelated elements in medieval literature, architecture, and painting, and this multeity has caused considerable difficulty for those who have sought to understand and explain the principles of medieval aesthetic unity. Medieval writers seem to have had few qualms about including a profusion of apparently heterogeneous elements in their works, and as a consequence many of their writings appear disunified by classical Greek and modern standards. Style and tone may vary throughout a work, verse and rhyme patterns may change, and plot lines may flow smoothly for a while, then stop, detour, and finally resume again.

Chaucer's *Canterbury Tales*, for example, seems disjunctive because of its diverse mixture of styles, genres, plots, and pilgrim narrators. His *Parlement of Foules* causes similar difficulties on a smaller scale as a result of its three separate sections, each different in narrative technique, style, genre, characterization, and description.[2] The English mystery play cycles, staged on separate wagons or scaffolds, display such a wide variety of styles, dramatic techniques, verse forms, and tones that they tempt us to consider each play out of context and to wonder whether the whole cycle has any unity or controlling design whatever. The question about the cycles is especially thorny because different authors wrote individual plays at different times, and some of the plays are fifty or more years older or younger than others in the same cycle. Medieval art, music, and architecture similarly display a mixture of heterogeneous elements. The great cathedrals, for example, blend comic gargoyles with serenely idealistic statues and unselfconsciously juxtapose early and late Gothic stylistic features.

This medieval fondness for weaving together diverse and apparently unrelated elements has been noted so often as to have become a critical commonplace. Such scholars as Heinrich Wölfflin, Arnold Hauser, Charles Muscatine, Eugéne Vinaver, R. M. Jordan, and William Ryding[3] have in one way or another reminded us that Gothic art reveals a picture of reality that "is like a panoramic survey, not a one-sided, unified representation, dominated by a single point of view."[4] There has been less agreement about how or even whether medieval artists conferred unity or harmony upon the multiplicity so often observed. Vinaver once commented that coherence in such medieval works is conveyed "through the amplification and expansion of the matter itself—a device which it will take the modern world nearly half-a-millennium to rediscover."[5] Jordan concludes his study of Chaucer's poetry with an explanation of medieval unity that's nearly as obscure as the principle itself: "In Chaucer we find art and belief coming together without merging. The result, to use Wölfflin's terms once more, is not a 'unified unity' but a 'multiple unity,' which allows each element full play and autonomy yet holds them together within a controlling outline."[6]

The principles of unity in medieval literature are elusive in part because we have been reluctant to let go of the obvious surface multiplicity and reach beyond it to the level of the design which underlies and supports the variety. As modern readers, we're accustomed to focusing initially on the meaning (the reality the poet refers to) and using it as the key to discover the organizing principle that underlies and supports it (the form through which the poet arranges the meaning). We may unconsciously feel that *Mankind*, or Chaucer's *Parlement of Foules* have some kind of unity, but we can't grasp the principle of that unity and abstract it from the given work because the superficial incompatibility of the various meanings blocks our accustomed approach to the form of each work. In short, by trying to understand the artistry in terms of the reality it refers to, we miss the structural reality of the art.

But when we do penetrate to the underlying structures, we are distracted by the great diversity, the inconsistencies of style, characterization, verse form, narrative technique, and so forth, that we encounter in literary works written between the twelfth and fifteenth centuries. The anonymous authors of *The Castle of Perseverance, Mankind*, and (to a lesser but still significant extent) *Wisdom* seem to have delighted in just this process, following and exaggerating the example of earlier medieval writers and purposely combining the most dissimilar elements in their individual plays.

But these Macro playwrights also are alike in the method they use to harmonize this multitude of heterogeneous elements, and in this too they may well be following the example of earlier writers. Each play elevates design (a different design in each case) to a place of prominence over all other elements and consistently applies that design to each of the various structural components that make up the work. In *The Castle of Perseverance*, every major structure displays a pattern of two-part repetition. In *Mankind*, the design causes the various structural components to undulate back and forth between the opposite poles of exposition and exemplification, abstraction and realism. In *Wisdom*, the controlling pattern is a mathematical scheme based on the number three and its various multiples. Because pattern dominates, the various structural components in each play resonate in an aesthetically pleasing harmony, a constructional consistency that is quite different from the more familiar organic unity found in the Western art of most other historical periods.

Successful works of art and literature produced in every period must, of course, have an ultimate principle of organization, a controlling design. What distinguishes much medieval art and literature from the art of other periods is the medieval emphasis on diversity in combination with the overwhelming dominance of design. Design triumphs over wide diversity, and art becomes one more means of satisfying the medieval desire to tidy up the universe, to order, codify, and systematize.[7]

We can call this emphasis on design in many medieval works of art and literature a constructional aesthetic. By emphasizing design, such an aesthetic depends far less on the homogeneity of the elements it arranges than on the consistent application of the design (whatever it might be) to each of the major structural components in a work. In fact, such a constructional emphasis is particularly effective in arranging essentially unrelated elements, and usually requires variety and multiplicity to fully succeed. Those audiences accustomed to looking for the design and taking pleasure in its consistent application would find the organizing pattern all the more pleasing when it arranges elements that are widely different from one another, since basically similar elements would not require a strong controlling design to harmonize them, and the constructional artistry would not be nearly as impressive. As long as the design subordinates other elements in a work, those elements can and generally should be markedly dissimilar, and as long as such dissimilarity exists, harmony, but not unity, will be the artistic achievement.

It's perhaps useful at this point to remind ourselves that a constructional aesthetic, though favored, wasn't the only kind of artistry used in the high Middle Ages. Aesthetically pleasing, unified works of literature and art that follow classical models also survive (Chaucer's *Miller's Tale*, for example), attesting to the range of artistic experimentation that was going on between the twelfth and the fifteenth centuries. We should remember as well that the number of medieval works surviving into the present is extremely limited, and that not all the chance survivors are equally fine, even by medieval standards of harmony. Thus, we must be careful not to formulate explanations of medieval aesthetics that account for the failures as if they were succeses, and we must be just as careful not to allow the surviving failures to cloud our attempts to understand the successes.

We might speculate briefly about what could have encouraged medieval writers and artists to choose an aesthetic emphasizing design. From the twelfth century on, artists and poets had the example of Scholastic philosophy, where pattern overtly brought order and harmony to apparently contradictory ideas drawn from faith, pagan and biblical sources, and reason.[8] During this same period, the advice of the manuals on poetry also favored arrangement and style over invention, since invention was considered a feature of both poetry and prose.[9] Writers also had the example of the four Evangelists who, in creating the New Testament, retold the major events of Christ's life in four separate ways, differing from one another not in doctrine—or so it was conventionally argued—but rather in arrangement and design. In his *Prologue* to the *Tale of*

Melibee, Chaucer justifies his retelling of a well-known story by an appeal to the example of the Evangelists. Since both the comedy and the sarcasm of Chaucer's justification gain a large measure of their force from the fact that his excuse is a naïve explanation of the obvious to his audience, Chaucer's citation of the Evangelists in such a context indicates that he assumed his audience would have understood and accepted their method. It's a method which involves retelling and reshaping the same basic story, where the differences between the four Evangelists, and hence the special artistry of each, lies "in hir tellyng" not in "hir sentence [their meaning]." [10]

The method of the four Gospels may well have encouraged the production of many literary works that were basically derivative in their ideas and meanings but creatively new in their style and arrangement—their imposition of pattern or design—a practice of retelling that the Macro plays clearly illustrate. The basic doctrine in each play and many of the characters and lines of dialogue are drawn from sermons or mystical treatises of the period, and the division of each play into the sequence of innocence/fall/redemption is based on and parallels the natural human condition as it was perceived in the Middle Ages. In the process of reshaping and restating the derivative and commonplace ideas, design naturally assumed a dominant position in these works, since it was primarily through design that each poet could display his talents as a maker.

Finally, the medieval view of the cosmos, refined in the twelfth century when Plato's *Timaeus* was "rediscovered," provided artists and writers of the Middle Ages with an ever-present illustration of how a consistent pattern could bring order and harmony to otherwise unrelated, heterogeneous elements. [11] In this model of the universe, the whole disparate range of creation is held in harmonious order and balance by the single and consistent force of God's own design—a rank ordering of every created thing into a rational hierarchy descending from the Creator to the lowest inanimate grain of sand. This Platonic, or more correctly, Pythagorean cosmos—viewed in the Middle Ages as God's own work of art—must have exerted a pervasive influence on every human creative endeavor. No man-made work could possibly include as wide a range of dissimilar elements as are found in Nature, and no way of harmonizing dissimilar elements would have been more appealing than God's way—the consistent triumph of design and order. This view of the cosmos continued to influence artists and writers in the Renaissance,[12] but the focus moved to man—the more homogeneous microcosm—and as a result we generally find somewhat less diversity and surface multeity in Renaissance art.

Recently, modern critics have successfully identified some medieval narrative or plot designs, recognizing interlace, bipartition, and even tripartition as types of narrative patterning.[13] Few attempts have yet been made, however, to determine if these narrative patterns extend to description, characterization, style, verse form, or the other minor structural components in literary works. Such studies are difficult because we lack experience in dealing with literary structures in terms of design—we are unaccustomed to recognizing how design functions on the levels of style, characterization, and so forth. In addition, we aren't very comfortable viewing a literary work as if it were some kind of electrical circuit or piece of mechanical engineering, and yet the example of other medieval artworks—the cathedrals, the polyphonic music, the diptychs and triptychs—strongly suggests that the medieval mind could conceive of an artwork as a collection of disparate elements harmonized by a pervasive design rather than a homogeneous blend, an organic unity.[14]

We can more readily trace the application of design through various structural levels in works like the Macro plays, written in flamboyant style, than in earlier medieval works, since as a late medieval mannerism, stylistic flamboyance exaggerates the differences among the various heterogeneous elements in a work and requires that the design holding those dissimilarities in harmony be more apparent, more dominant on every level. Unless the design is almost mechanically pervasive, the exaggerated elements of the flamboyant duality would collapse into a jumbled heap. The taste for these extremes caused writers in the fifteenth century to blur the distinction between art and engineering, and poets, such as those who wrote the Macro plays, so emphasize design that their works seem like little machines. But fifteenth-century art-as-engineering differs really only in degree from the art of Chaucer, the art of Guillaume de Loris and Jean de Meun, or the art of Chrétien de Troyes. All celebrate design. The fifteenth-century poets differ primarily in the extent to which they carry their celebration.

By celebrating design, each of the Macro plays is able to present a multitude of diverse surfaces for contemplation. We can derive additional enjoyment from them (and from many other medieval literary works as well) when we simultaneously perceive the diversity and the constructional consistency of the particular design that arranges and disposes it on each structural level in each work. The three plays are microcosmic mirrors of the medieval cosmos. Each is drawn by a principle of consistent structural organization into a harmoniously tuned polyphony of dissimilar, yet interrelated elements—a balance of sameness and difference—that produces the pleasure of a well-made work of art and the delight of a puzzle solved.

Richly various, filled with surprising juxtapositions, the flamboyant Macro moralities please us as dramatic spectacles and possibly show us how to understand and appreciate some earlier medieval works as well. They are moral plays to be sure, but today their message is as much about beauty as it is about goodness and truth.

Notes & Index

Notes

CHAPTER I. Introduction

1. Robert A. Potter, *The English Morality Play: Origins, History and Influence of a Dramatic Tradition* (London: Routledge & Kegan Paul, 1975), p. 8. Others besides Potter have recognized this basic sequence, but his is the most thorough treatment of it. The third stage might also be called "repentance" or "restoration."
2. In *Non-Cycle Plays and Fragments*, ed. Norman Davis, Early English Text Society Supplementary Text 1 (London: Oxford University Press, 1970).
3. In *Everyman and Medieval Miracle Plays*, ed. A. C. Cawley (New York: E. P. Dutton, 1959).
4. Potter, *English Morality Plays*, p. 2.
5. In *English Morality Plays and Moral Interludes*, ed. Edgar T. Schell and J. D. Shuchter (New York: Holt, Rinehart and Winston, 1969).
6. In *Specimens of the Pre-Shakespearian Drama*, ed. John Matthews Manly (Boston and New York: Ginn and Co., 1903–4), vol. 1.
7. Potter, *English Morality Plays*, pp. 30–31, considers these three early sixteenth-century moralities to be medieval, bringing his total of medieval moralities to eight. Carl J. Stratman, *Bibliography of Medieval Drama* (Berkeley: University of California Press, 1954), also lists these three as medieval moralities and expands his list with many other sixteenth-century plays. The question, of

course, is when the Middle Ages ended in England (a perfectly legitimate point for debate which I will not argue here). For a full discussion of the generic criteria of the moralities (medieval and Renaissance), see Potter, pp. 8–33.

8. Editions of the three plays are invariably called *The Macro Plays* or *The Macro Moralities*, and libraries often don't cross-reference the individual titles, making retrieval of the texts by anyone except a serious medievalist next to impossible.

9. William Hone, *Ancient Mysteries Described* (London: Printed for W. Hone, 1823), p. x.

10. Thomas Sharp, *A Dissertation on the Pageants or Dramatic Mysteries Anciently Performed at Coventry* (Coventry: Merridew and Son, 1825), p. 23.

11. *The Macro Plays*, ed., F. J. Furnivall and Alfred W. Pollard, Early English Text Society, Extra Series 91 (London: K. Paul, Trench, Trübner and Co., Ltd., 1904).

12. Potter, *English Morality Plays*, p. 232.

13. *The Macro Plays*, ed. Mark Eccles, Early English Text Society 262 (London: Oxford University Press, 1969), p. xxiv. Eccles notes, p. xxiv, that Nevill Coghill saw a production of *The Castle of Perseverance* in Windsor in 1939, and quotes Coghill as saying: "Above all it revealed what an excellent and actable play it is, full of character, variety, and excitement." An unsigned review of the Experimental Theatre Club's performance of the play at Oxford appears in the *Oxford Magazine*, 17 November 1938, p. 170.

14. Eccles, *Macro Plays*, p. xxviii.

15. Ibid., pp. xi, xxxi, xxxviii. Eccles leaves the question of Norfolk or Suffolk open, since the handwriting has characteristics of both and the text of *Mankind* contains

references to locations in Cambridgeshire, Suffolk, and Norfolk.

16. Macro was a native of Bury St. Edmunds, see Eccles, *Macro Plays*, p. vii.

17. The educational level of many friars and most parish priests in the fifteenth century was little more than adequate, yet these three plays are highly sophisticated in their treatment of moral theology.

18. This assessment arises out of the modern prejudice against allegory. Some who have made the observation are: Henry Hitch Adams, *English Domestic or Homilectic Tragedy*, Columbia University Studies in English and Comparative Literature, no. 159 (New York, 1943), p. 56; Katherine Lee Bates, *The English Religious Drama* (London: Macmillan, 1917), p. 202; C. F. Tucker Brooke, *Tudor Drama* (Boston: Houghton, 1911), p. 51; Alan S. Downer, *The British Drama* (New York: Appleton-Century-Crofts, Inc., 1950), p. 189; John Speirs, "A Survey of Medieval Verse," in *The Pelican Guide to English Literature*, ed. Boris Ford (Baltimore: Penguin Books, 1966), p. 61; Donald Clive Stuart, *The Development of Dramatic Art* (New York: Dover, 1960), p. 189. Many others have made similar observations.

19. O. B. Hardison, *Christian Rite and Christian Drama in the Middle Ages* (Baltimore: Johns Hopkins University Press, 1965), pp. 18, 20, and 21, points out that the major scholars of medieval drama in the first half of this century—E. K. Chambers, John Matthews Manly, and Karl Young—were strongly influenced by the analogy between biological and literary development. Their views affected many others as well. For a survey of critical attitudes about the moralities, see Potter, *English Morality Plays*, pp. 192–221.

20. Hardin Craig, *English Religious Drama of the Middle Ages* (1955; reprint ed., Oxford: Clarendon Press, 1968), p. 350.

21. E. K. Chambers, *English Literature at the Close of the Middle Ages* (1945; reprint ed., Oxford: Clarendon Press, 1957), p. 61.

22. Craig, *English Religious Drama*, p. 350.

23. Stanley Kahrl, *Traditions of Medieval English Drama* (Pittsburgh: University of Pittsburgh Press, 1975), pp. 106–7.

24. See A. Abram, *English Life and Manners in the Later Middle Ages* (London: George Routledge & Sons, Ltd., 1913), pp. 170–71; Erich Auerbach, *Mimesis: The Representation of Reality in Western Literature*, trans. Willard Trask (1946; reprint ed., Princeton: Princeton University Press, 1968), pp. 232, 259; Helmut Hatzfeld, "La littérature flamboyante au XVe siècle," in *Studi in onore di Carlo Pellegrini* (Rome: Socicta Editrice Internazionale, 1963), 2:82; Hatzfeld, *Literature through Art: A New Approach to French Literature* (New York: Oxford University Press, 1952), p. 38; J. Huizinga, *The Waning of the Middle Ages* (1924; reprint ed., New York: Doubleday Anchor, 1954), pp. 94, 101, 248.

25. Hatzfeld, "La littérature flamboyante," p. 81.

26. H. Pirenne, G. Cohen, Henri Focillon, *La civilisation occidentale au moyen âge* (Paris: Les Presses Universitaires de France, 1933), p. 630. Paraphrased in Hatzfeld, "La littérature flamboyante," p. 81.

27. Huizinga, *Waning of the Middle Ages*, p. 209.

28. Ibid., p. 274.

29. See Hugh T. Broadley, *Flemish Painting in the National Gallery of Art* (Washington, D.C.: National Gallery of Art, 1960), p. 12; and Huizinga, *Waning of the Middle Ages*, pp. 278–79.

30. Huizinga, *Waning of the Middle Ages*, p. 264.
31. Sermons of the period offer particularly good examples of this. See *Middle English Sermons*, ed. Woodburn O. Ross, Early English Text Society, o.s. 209 (London: Oxford University Press, 1940).
32. *Jacob's Well*, ed. Arthur Brandeis, Early English Text Society, o.s. 115 (London: Kegan Paul, 1900).
33. Ibid., p. 185. I have modernized the language somewhat.
34. Charles Muscatine, *Chaucer and the French Tradition* (1957; reprint ed., Berkeley: University of California Press, 1966), p. 12.
35. Ibid., p. 59.　　　　36. Ibid., pp. 58–59.
37. Ibid., pp. 11, 58.　　38. Ibid., pp. 96–97, 223.
39. Auerbach, *Mimesis*, pp. 151, 153.
40. Ibid., pp. 242–43; Muscatine, *Chaucer and the French Tradition*, p. 245.
41. Auerbach, *Mimesis*, p. 248.
42. R. T. Davies, ed., *Medieval English Lyrics* (Evanston, Ill.: Northwestern University Press, 1967), p. 211.
43. Ibid., p. 86.
44. Huizinga, *Waning of the Middle Ages*, p. 213.
45. Aside from the allegory, *Jacob's Well* is written in a rather unadorned style; the work is typical of many written during this period. See Brandeis, *Jacob's Well*, p. vi.
46. *The Prologues and Epilogues of William Caxton*, ed. W. J. B. Crotch, Early English Text Society, o.s. 176 (London: Oxford University Press, 1928), p. 37.
47. H. S. Bennett, *Chaucer and the Fifteenth Century* (Oxford: Clarendon Press, 1965), p. 116.
48. Hatzfeld, "La littérature flamboyante," p. 81.
49. Huizinga, *Waning of the Middle Ages*, p. 138.
50. James M. Clark, *The Dance of Death in the Middle Ages and the Renaissance* (Glasgow: Jackson, 1950), p. 2.
51. An edition of the *Disputacion Betwyx the Body and*

Wormes is provided by Karl Brunner, "Mittelenglische Todesgeschichte," *Archiv für das Studium der neueren Sprachen und Literaturen* 167 (1935): 30 ff. For additional pictures of tombstones and a study of the changing attitudes toward death in the late Middle Ages, see Kathleen Cohen, *Metamorphosis of a Death Symbol* (Berkeley: University of California Press, 1973).

52. See *The Book of the Craft of Dying*, ed. Francis Comper (1917; reprint ed., New York: Arno Press, 1977), and Huizinga, *Waning of the Middle Ages*, p. 147.

53. Huizinga, *Waning of the Middle Ages*, p. 146.

54. In Davies, *Medieval English Lyrics*, p. 251.

55. *The Book of Vices and Virtues*, ed. W. Nelson Francis, Early English Text Society, o.s. 217 (London: Oxford University Press, 1942), p. ix.

56. See Potter, *English Morality Plays*, pp. 17–20.

57. John Lydgate, *The Assembly of Gods*, ed. Oscar Triggs, Early English Text Society, Extra Series 69 (London: Kegan Paul, Trench, Trübner, 1896), pp. lxix–lxxii.

58. Francis, *The Book of Vices and Virtues*, p. ix.

59. G. R. Owst, *Literature and Pulpit in Medieval England* (1933; reprint ed., Oxford: Basil Blackwell, 1966), pp. 315–19. Sermons, satires, complaints, dramas, allegories, all inveighed against avarice in the fifteenth century.

60. Hope Traver, "The Four Daughters of God" (Ph.D. diss., Bryn Mawyr College, 1907), pp. 162–63.

61. Potter, *English Morality Plays*, pp. 3–4, draws an interesting distinction between the "illusionistic theatre" and the "presentational theatre."

62. Karl Young, *The Drama of the Medieval Church* (Oxford: Clarendon Press, 1933), 1:80–81.

63. Potter, *English Morality Plays*, p. 16, sees the moralities as

"theatre of demonstration" and as ritual. I agree with the former, but not the latter.

64. The view was expressed early in this century by E. N. S. Thompson, "The English Moral Plays," *Transactions of the Connecticut Academy of Arts and Sciences* 14 (New Haven, 1910): 320. Thompson used the Latin term "sermo corporeus" to describe the moralities. The term has been translated, and unfortunately, often repeated.

CHAPTER 2. Circles within Circles
The Castle of Perseverance

1. See David M. Bevington, *From "Mankind" to Marlowe* (Cambridge, Mass.: Harvard University Press, 1962), p. 72. Bevington supposes (p. 49) that role-doubling was not used in the production of this play.

2. See Jacob Bennett, "A Linguistic Study of *The Castle of Perseverance*" (Ph.D. diss., Boston University, 1960). In his dissertation, and in an article based on it, "*The Castle of Perseverance*: Redactions, Place and Date," *Medieval Studies* 24 (1962): 141–52, Bennett uses the criteria of meter, alliteration, style, grammar, syntax, and dramatic effectiveness to support his contention that there are two redactions to the play. One of these is the twelve-stanza speech of the heralds, the other the closing sequence involving the Four Daughters of God. Eccles, in his edition of *The Macro Plays* pp. xiv–xvii, disagrees with Bennett's view that the Four Daughters of God sequence was written by someone other than the author of the rest of the play, but agrees that another

author probably composed the banns. I am inclined to support Eccles's position.

3. In my quotations from the play, I have chosen to follow the practice of the manuscript's scribe and not indent every other line, although Eccles does so in his edition for the Early English Text Society, which I am using for all quotations from the plays.

4. Hatzfeld, "La littérature flamboyante," p. 95.

5. See Richard Southern, *The Medieval Theatre in the Round*, rev. ed. (New York: Theatre Arts Books, 1975), pp. 153, 165, 208. Southern provides a fascinating re-creation of the play's performance and staging.

6. See Bartlett J. Whiting, *Proverbs in the Earlier English Drama* (1938; reprint ed., New York: Octogon Books, 1969), pp. 68–69.

7. Both Bennett, "Redactions, Place and Date," p. 142, and Eccles, *Macro Plays*, p. xviii, have noted this division of meaning in the stanzas. Using terms borrowed from discussions of the sonnet, Bennett calls the two parts exposition and conclusion.

8. For in-depth treatments of this linguistic device, see John Allan Conley, "Four Studies in Aureate Terms" (Ph.D. diss., Stanford University, 1956); John Cooper Mendenhall, "Aureate Terms, A Study in the Literary Diction of the Fifteenth Century" (Ph.D. diss., University of Pennsylvania, 1919).

9. Marianne Grier Briscoe, "The Relation of Medieval Preaching Manuals to the Medieval English Morality Plays" (Ph.D. diss., Catholic University of America, 1975), p. 132.

10. Southern, *Medieval Theatre in the Round*, p. 165. Southern finds this speech, and the ones by Mankind and Death when they first enter the arena, to be filled with ref-

erences to walking and wending, suggesting that they were delivered processionally.

11. Ibid., p. 208.

12. Thomas Aquinas, *Summa Theologica* (Part 1, Question 113, Article 2, and Part 1, Question 114, Article 1). For an English translation see *Summa Theologica*, trans. Fathers of the English Dominican Province (New York: Benziger Bros., 1947), 1:550–59.

CHAPTER 3. Exposition and Illustration: *Mankind*

1. In quoting from the play, I again follow the manuscript practice of not indenting every other line, rather than Eccles's practice, whose edition of the play I have used for all quotations.

2. Sister Mary Philippa Coogan, *An Interpretation of the Moral Play "Mankind"* (Washington, D.C.: Catholic University of America Press, 1947), p. 59.

3. A leaf is missing in the original manuscript following line 71, shortly after Mischief first enters, but it's not likely that he and the three rogues introduced themselves in the seventy or so lines that are now lost. If they did, it would make Mercy's question about the names of the three rogues at line 114 irrelevant and would make Mischief's reminder to the audience at line 417 that he was on stage at the beginning of the play equally unnecessary. Judging from the overwhelming sermonizing dominance of Mercy in this first part of the play, it's far more likely that he, rather than any of the four rogues, spoke the lines that are now lost.

4. See *O.E.D.* In the Wakefield or Towneley Cycle "Last Judgment," Tutivillus carries a bag or sack (225), though

here he has collected a variety of different kinds of sinners. When asked by a fellow demon to identify himself, Tutivillus responds in somewhat garbled Latin, saying he strings together scraps of words (after 250). *The Towneley Plays*, ed. George England and Alfred W. Pollard, Early English Text Society, Extra Series 71 (1897; reprint ed., Oxford: Oxford University Press, 1966), pp. 374–75.

5. See Coogan, *An Interpretation*, pp. 6–7, 14–15.

6. Bevington, *From "Mankind" to Marlowe*, pp. 72, 87.

7. The likelihood of an indoor performance gives support to the view, expressed by Sister Philippa Coogan, *An Interpretation*, pp. 1–56, and by W. K. Smart, "Some Notes on *Mankind*," pp. 45–58, that *Mankind* was written as a Shrovetide or Lenten play, since early spring weather would not be particularly hospitable to an outdoor production. There's nothing in the play so completely linking it to Shrovetide that it couldn't be performed at other times in the year as well, and it's risky to assume that a play with Lenten allusions would have been performed only at Lent—just as risky and unsupportable, say, as a contention that *The Canterbury Tales* was written to be read in April.

8. T. W. Craik, *The Tudor Interlude: Stage, Costume, and Acting* (Leicester: University of Leicester Press, 1958), p. 9.

9. Coogan, *An Interpretation*, p. 7, accepts L. W. Cushman's theory that Mercy is costumed as a Dominican friar, "The Devil and the Vice in the English Dramatic Literature Before Shakespeare," *Studien zur Englischen Philologie* (Halle: Max Niemeyer, 1900), 6:85. If Cushman's theory is correct, Mercy would probably be dressed in the robe and cowl of a Dominican rather than in a cas-

sock and surplice. I think there's little doubt that he was dressed as some kind of cleric.

10. Coogan, *An Interpretation*, pp. 63–64.

11. An early editor of *Mankind*, Alois Brandl, *Quellen des Weltlichen Dramas in England vor Shakespeare* (Strassborg: Trübner, 1898), p. xxxiii, supposed that Mischief was dressed as a farmer, since he refers to himself (54) as a winter corn thresher. At the other extreme, Robert Ramsay, in the introduction to his edition of John Skelton's *Magnygycence*, Early English Text Society, Extra Series 98 (London: K. Paul, Trench, Trübner and Co., Ltd., 1906), p. cxciv, surmises that Mischief, like Titivillus, wore a devil's outfit. Brandl's position at least has some support from the text of the play.

12. In his edition of *Mankind*, anthologized in *Medieval Drama* (Boston: Houghton Mifflin Company, 1975), pp. 901–38, David Bevington adds a stage direction (after 630) inexplicably indicating that besides church furnishings, Nowadays has stolen the Sacrament. Apart from the fact that there seems nothing in the text to support this, it would appear to be most unlikely that such blasphemy would be allowed even in the Middle Ages.

13. This view was especially prevalent among early commentators. See *The Macro Plays*, ed. F. J. Furnivall and Alfred W. Pollard, Early English Text Society, Extra Series 91 (London: K. Paul, Trench, Trübner and Co., Ltd., 1904), pp. xi–xii; Walter Kay Smart, "Some Notes on *Mankind*," *Modern Philology* 14 (1916): 312; Coogan, *An Interpretation*, p. 95; Hardin Craig, *English Religious Drama of the Middle Ages*, p. 343. Eccles, *Macro Plays*, p. xlv, thought it written for "the common people." The view is not now as popular, see Stanley Kahrl, *Traditions of Medieval English Drama*, p. 115; Lawrence

Clopper, "*Mankind* and Its Audience," *Comparative Drama* 9 (1974–75): 347–55. Clopper brings the discussion around full circle, unconvincingly contending that *Mankind* was possibly written for "a private audience of intelligentsia" p. 353.

14. See Eccles, *Macro Plays*, note to line 73, p. 217.
15. Walter Kay Smart, "*Mankind* and the Mummers' Play," *Modern Language Notes* 32 (1917): 21.
16. Coogan, *An Interpretation*, p. 104.
17. See Smart, "Some Notes on *Mankind*," p. 312; J. Q. Adams, *Chief Pre-Shakespearean Dramas* (Boston: Houghton Mifflin, 1924), p. 304, n.; Hardin Craig, *English Religious Drama*, p. 343; Arnold Williams, *The Drama of Medieval England* (East Lansing: Michigan State University Press, 1961), p. 155. A recent study seeks to redeem *Mankind* by demonstrating its artistic use of the story of Job: Lorraine Stock, "Thematic and Structural Unity in *Mankind*," *Studies in Philology* 72 (1975): 121–35.

CHAPTER 4. Number as Design: *Wisdom*

1. Two rather thorough studies of *Wisdom*'s style have been produced by Sister Christian Koontz: "The Duality of Styles in the Morality Play *Wisdom Who is Christ*: A Classical-Rhetorical Analysis," *Style* 7 (1973): 251–70, and "A Stylistic Analysis of the Morality Play *Wisdom Who is Christ*" (Ph.d. diss., Catholic University of America, 1971). In this and my other quotations from *Wisdom*, I again follow the original manuscript practice of not indenting lines, rather than Eccles's edition.
2. The Gospel texts, in the Rheims translation, are Matt. 22: 36–40, Mark 12:29–31, and Luke 10:27–28. The *Wis-*

dom poet follows this and his other known sources almost to the letter. For a full source study see Walter Kay Smart, *Some English and Latin Sources and Parallels for the Morality of Wisdom* (Menasha, Wisconsin: George Banta Publishing Co., 1912). Additional explication of the source of *Wisdom*'s allegory is provided by Eugene Hill, "The Trinitarian Allegory of the Moral Play *Wisdom*," *Modern Philology* 73 (1975): 121–35.

3. For discussions of the contemporary satire in this section of *Wisdom*, see David Bevington, "Political Satire in the Morality *Wisdom Who is Christ*," *Renaissance Papers 1963* (Durham, N.C.: Duke University Press, 1964), pp. 41–51; Milton McC. Gatch, "Mysticism and Satire in the Morality of *Wisdom*," *Philological Quarterly* 53 (1974): 342–62.

4. John J. Molloy, *A Theological Interpretation of the Moral Play "Wisdom, Who is Christ"* (Washington, D.C.: Catholic University of America Press, 1952), p. 188. While he recognizes this more positive approach in *Wisdom*'s moral message, Molloy still feels the play was written for laymen.

5. Smart, *Some English and Latin Sources*, pp. 79–86, argues that *Wisdom* was written for an audience of monks, probably at Bury St. Edmunds. Molloy, *Theological Interpretation*, pp. 198–215, argues directly against Smart and maintains that *Wisdom* was intended for laymen. Bevington, "Political Satire," thought that *Wisdom* was written to reform monastics, to make them give up politics and return to their monasteries. In her dissertation, Sister Christian Koontz argues that *Wisdom* was intended to be performed by monks for monks, p. 151. The debate is not likely to be settled. Gatch, "Mysticism and Satire," claims that *Wisdom* "is clearly directed to a lay audience," p. 362.

6. See Dom David Knowles, *The Religious Orders in England* (Cambridge: Cambridge University Press, 1957), 2:258. Bury had sixty monks around the year 1500, which made it second only to Canterbury's seventy monks. Other abbeys with forty or more monks included St. Albans, Gloucester, Westminster, Ely, and Reading. According to Knowles, p. 258: "No other order, taken over the whole [medieval] period, could come within sight of such totals." In *From "Mankind" to Marlowe*, David Bevington surmises that *Wisdom* was taken on tour and could be performed by a troupe of five or six actors and six mute boys, p. 125. Merle Fifield, "The Use of Doubling and 'Extras' in *Wisdom, Who is Christ*," *Ball State University Forum* 6 (1965): 65–68, explains that the play could be performed by six professional actors, a minstrel, and local nonprofessionals who could perform in the dances and processions. Eccles, *Macro Plays*, p. xxxv, supposes that if the dances were omitted, *Wisdom* could be performed by six men and seven boys.

7. In her dissertation, "Duality of Styles," Sister Christian Koontz mentions in passing that *Wisdom* "might . . . have been written as a paraliturgical service . . . for nonprofessional performance as a religious activity," p. 151. I believe the text of the play supports her view.

8. Eccles, *Macro Plays*, p. xxx.

9. Augustine, *De Musica*, trans. Robert C. Taliaferro, in *The Writings of St. Augustine* (New York: CIMA Publishing, Inc., 1947), II: 151–379. Augustine's comment on the perfection of the number three is in Bk. 1, chap. 12, sec. 20: "So you see there is a certain perfection in three because it is a whole: it has a beginning, middle and an end."

10. S. K. Heninger, Jr., *Touches of Sweet Harmony: Pythagorean Cosmology and Renaissance Poetics* (San Marino,

Calif.: Huntington Library, 1974), p. 84. Much of what Heninger says about the Renaissance view of the cosmos applies, of course, to the medieval view as well.

11. 1 John 2:16.

12. See Molloy, *Theological Interpretation*, pp. 100–131.

13. The visual motif of seven devils leaving a sinful soul occurs in at least two other medeival plays as a bit of stage business: the *Digby Mary Magdalene* (s.d. after 691), and the *Ludus Coventriae* "Last Supper" (495–505). *The Digby Plays*, ed. F. J. Furnivall, Early English Text Society, Extra Series 71 (1896; reprint ed., Oxford: Oxford University Press, 1967); *Ludus Coventriae or The Plaie Called Corpus Christi*, ed. K. S. Block, Early English Text Society, Extra Series 120 (1922; reprint ed., Oxford: Oxford University Press, 1960).

14. Smart, *Some English and Latin Sources*, p. 34, says the source of this sermon on the nine points pleasing to God is the Latin *Novem Virtutes*, attributed to the mystic Richard Rolle.

CHAPTER 5. Art as Design

1. The concept of an aesthetic structure as one of relations simply as such is developed by J. Craig LaDrière, "Literary Form and Form in the Other Arts," *Stil-und Formprobleme in Der Literatur* (Heidelberg: Carl Winter, 1959), pp. 28–37, and especially p. 32. LaDrière's theory of literary aesthetics has greatly influenced me, and it seems particularly suited to medieval literature. For further discussion, see his "Structure, Sound, and Meaning," in *Sound and Poetry: English Institute Essays, 1956*, ed. Northrup Frye (New York: Columbia University Press, 1957), pp. 85–108, and his articles, "Classifi-

cation," "Form," "Scientific Method in Criticism," and "Voice and Address" in *The Dictionary of World Literature,* ed. Joseph Shipley (1953; reprint ed., Totowa, N.J.: Littlefield, Adams & Co., 1966).

2. I have applied my concept of a constructional aesthetic, outlined in this chapter and underlying my study of the three Macro plays throughout this volume, to Chaucer's *Parlement of Foules* and found that the rhetorical ornament, antithesis, is the organizational pattern for each major structural component in that work. My findings were presented in 1976 at the Eleventh Conference on Medieval Studies at Western Michigan University, Kalamazoo, in a paper entitled "Constructional Harmony in Chaucer's *Parlement of Foules.*" An expanded version of that paper will be published as an article, "Antithesis as the Principle of Design in the *Parlement of Foules,*" *Chaucer Review,* in press.

3. See Heinrich Wölfflin, *Kunstgeschichtliche Grundbegriffe* (Munich: F. Bruckmann, 1915), pp. 167–210; Arnold Hauser, *The Social History of Art,* trans. Stanley Godman (New York: Random House, 1951), 1:272–73; Charles Muscatine, *Chaucer and the French Tradition* (1957; reprint ed., Berkeley: University of California Press, 1966), pp. 167–69; Eugène Vinaver, "À la recherche d'une poétique médiévale," *Cahiers de civilisation médiévale* 2 (1959): 1–16, and "Form and Meaning in Medieval Romance," The Presidential Address of the Modern Humanities Research Association (Leeds: MHRA, 1966), p. 13; Robert M. Jordan, *Chaucer and the Shape of Creation* (Cambridge, Mass.: Harvard University Press, 1967), p. 43; William Ryding, *Structure in Medieval Narrative* (The Hague: Mouton, 1971), p. 116. This is, of course, only a partial listing of scholars who

have noted the multeity and apparent disjunctiveness of medieval art and literature.

4. Hauser, *Social History of Art*, 1:273, cited by Muscatine, *Chaucer and the French Tradition*, p. 167.
5. Vinaver, "Form and Meaning," p. 13.
6. *Chaucer and the Shape of Creation*, p. 241.
7. C. S. Lewis, *Studies in Medieval and Renaissance Literature* (Cambridge: Cambridge University Press, 1966), pp. 44–45.
8. Erwin Panofsky, *Gothic Architecture and Scholasticism* (New York: Meridian Books, 1957), pp. 34–35. Panofsky deals at length with the influences of the Scholastic method on art and architecture throughout this volume.
9. *Poetria Nova of Geoffrey of Vinsauf*, trans. Margaret Nims (Toronto: Pontifical Institute of Mediaeval Studies, 1967), p. 10. Douglas Kelly, "Theory of Composition in Medieval Narrative Poetry and Geoffrey of Vinsauf's *Poetria Nova*," *Mediaeval Studies* 31 (1969): 127, notes that Geoffrey "metaphorically considered [poetic composition] analogous to the planning and construction of a building" and adds that Geoffrey's influence was extensive.
10. See Chaucer's *Prologue to The Tale of Melibee* (943–66). *The Works of Geoffrey Chaucer*, ed. F. N. Robinson (Boston: Houghton Mifflin Co., 1961), p. 167.
11. Chalcidius's Latin translation of the *Timaeus* was known before the twelfth century, but the work's strong influence on medieval thought began in the twelfth century. Plato, *Timaeus*, trans. H. D. P. Lee (Baltimore: Penguin Books, 1965).
12. See S. K. Heninger, *Touches of Sweet Harmony: Pythagorean Cosmology and Renaissance Poetics* (San Marino, Calif.: Huntington Library, 1974), pp. 327, 340. The ob-

servations Heninger makes about influences on Renaissance poetics are equally applicable to the Middle Ages.

13. See Vinaver, "Form and Meaning," pp. 17–22; Ryding, *Structure*, p. 116.

14. See Vinaver, "Form and Meaning," 13; Jordan, *Chaucer*, pp. 236 ff.

Index

Abstinence: character in *Castle of Perseverance*, 29, 48, 49. *See also* Virtues

Abstractions, allegorical: dramatic difficulties with, 22–23, 25; portrayed by live actors in plays, 22, 35–36, 71, 103; mixed with semifictional characters in *Mankind*, 76–77. *See also* High style elements

Abstract language: in *Mankind*, 65; in *Wisdom*, 97. *See also* High style elements

Actions: illustrative of doctrine in *Mankind*, 83, 88–89; nearly none in *Wisdom*, 96

Actors: in *Castle of Perseverance*, 35, 36; in *Mankind*, 78; in *Wisdom*, 105

Admission fee: possible, in *Castle of Perseverance*, 30; earliest reference to in an English play (*Mankind*), 79–80

Adultery: character in *Wisdom*, 102

Aesthetic principles: of medieval literature, 4–18 passim; of *Castle of Perseverance*, 62–63; of *Mankind*, 90–93; of *Wisdom*, 96, 106–18; multeity vs. unity, 121–28. *See also* Constructional aesthetic

Allegorical: characters in Macro plays, 4; characterizations, 22–23; abstractions portrayed by live actors in plays, 22, 35–36, 71, 103; motifs in *Mankind*, 69; mind-set of fifteenth century, 76; concepts mixed with semifictional characters in *Mankind*, 76–77

Allegory: religious, xiii; dramatized, 1; mixed with realism in flamboyant style, 12; delight in, 16; moral, in *Wisdom*, 108

Alliteration: as ornamentation in *Castle of Perseverance*, 42

Alternation: as design in *Mankind*, 82–93. *See also* Design; Principle of organization

Amplification: through repetition in *Castle of Perseverance*, 39–42, 45, 56; in *Wisdom*, 98–100. *See also* Repetition

Angels: parallel story to Mankind's in *Castle of Perseverance*, 60. *See also* Bad Angel; Good Angel

Anger: character in *Castle of Perseverance*, 36; in *Wisdom*, 102. *See also* Seven Deadly Sins

Anima: character in *Wisdom*, as soul of man, 94; taught by Wisdom, 95; uses aureate terms, 97;

Index

uses same stanza form as Wisdom, 100; costume, 101, 103, 113; makes nine requests, 107; presents litany in legal form, 109; makes confession, 114; duality of flawed soul, 115; nine aspects of, 115; mentioned, 96, 98, 99, 104, 113, 116
Annunciation, The: Flemish painting by Jan Van Eyck, 9, 10, 14
Antithesis: as principle of organization in *Parlement of Foules*, 146n2
Aristocracy: as patrons of literature, 17–18
Ars moriendi (art of dying): as literary genre, 20
Art: visual, 9–11, 122, 124; as design, 119; as disparate elements harmonized by design, 127; -as-engineering in fifteenth century, 128. *See also* Principle of organization
Artistic: evaluation, xiv; design of *Mankind*, 86; experimentation in Middle Ages, 125
Audience: for Macro plays, 27; as influence on structure of *Castle of Perseverance*, 37, 44, 45, 48, 52; of *Mankind*, 75; participation in, 78–79; socially mixed, 81–82; of clerics for *Wisdom*, 104–5, 109, 111
Aureate terms: defined, 42; used sparingly in *Castle of Perseverance*, 42; used in *Mankind*, 65–68; as extensive decoration in *Wisdom*, 96–99; effect

heightened by rhyme position, 97
Avarice: special attention to, 21; triumphant vice in *Castle of Perseverance*, 51; fifteenth-century view of, 136n59. *See also* Seven Deadly Sins
Ayenbite of Inwyt (Dan Michel), 21

Backbiter: character in *Castle of Perseverance*, 30, 36–37, 45, 48, 51
Bad Angel (and Good Angel): characters in *Castle of Perseverance*, 30, 37, 44–45, 48–49, 51–52, 56–60
Banns: in *Castle of Perseverance*, 30
Battle: in *Castle of Perseverance*, 49–51; between soul and body in *Mankind*, 74
Belyal: devil in *Castle of Perseverance*, 32, 37, 46, 58; with his props, 35–36. *See also* World, Flesh, and the Devil
Benedictines: possible use of drama as device for religious instruction, 4. *See also* Bury St. Edmunds
Biblical quotations: used in *Castle of Perseverance*, 43
Black Plague (ca. 1348), 17, 18
Bourgeoisie, 17–18
Bourgeois realism. *See* Realism
Bury St. Edmunds: Benedictine abbey and town in Suffolk, possible origin of Macro manuscript, 3–4; *Wisdom* probably

Index

severance, 36, 102. *See also* Seven Deadly Sins

Evangelists, Four: arrangements of Christ's life differ, 125; cited as artistic example by Chaucer, 126

Everyman (ca. 1500): first modern staging (1901), 2; differs from *Mankind*, 90; mentioned, 24, 126

Exaggeration: of opposites in flamboyant works, 9, 13–18, 128; fifteenth-century artistic, in Macro plays, 120–21. *See also* Ornamentation

Exemplification. *See* Perceptual example

Falseness: character in *Wisdom*, 102

Figuration. *See* High style elements

Five Wits. *See* Wits, Five

Flamboyant: characteristics of style, 5; Franco-Burgundian origins, 8; ornamentation in, 9, 28; combination of allegory and realism, 11, 12, 13, 14, 17, 18, 22; as medieval mannerism, 18, 128; in *Castle of Perseverance*, 32–55, 62–63; in *Mankind*, 65–77, 93; in *Wisdom*, 95–104; blend provides spectacle and also reinforces message, 104; exaggeration of, in Macro plays, 120–21, 128. *See also* High style elements; Ornamentation; Realism

Flemish painting, 9

Flesh. *See* World, Flesh, and the Devil

Folly: character in *Castle of Perseverance*, 30

Fornication: character in *Wisdom*, 102

Four Daughters of God. *See* Daughters of God, Four

French inverted word order: as decoration in *Wisdom*, 96–97

Garcio ("boy"): character in *Castle of Perseverance*, 30, 52

Generosity: character in *Castle of Perseverance*, 29, 49, 51. *See also* Virtues

Genre: of *Wisdom*, paraliturgical masque, 104–5, 144n7

Gesta Romanorum (fourteenth century), 22

Gluttony: character in *Castle of Perseverance*, 36; character in *Wisdom*, 103. *See also* Seven Deadly Sins

God: as character in *Castle of Perseverance*, 30, 53, 54

Good Angel (and Bad Angel): characters in *Castle of Perseverance*, 30, 37, 44–45, 48–49, 51–52, 56–60

Gospels: as examples for medieval art, 126. *See also* Evangelists, Four

Gothic style: in cathedral architecture, 8; as multiplicity, 122. *See also* High style elements

Gower, John: fourteenth-century writer, 20, 120

Index

Law courts: abuses parodied in
Wisdom, 102
Lechery: character in *Castle of
Perseverance*, 23, 36, 49, 102;
major sin in *Wisdom*, 111; three
phases of, in *Wisdom*, 112. See
also Seven Deadly Sins
Litany: in legal format in *Wisdom*, 109
Lollards, 27
Loris, Guillame de, 128
Lucifer, Prince of Darkness (Devil): tempter in *Wisdom*, 95;
stanza form used, 100–101; grabs
small boy, 105; speaks, 110–12;
mentioned, 104, 116. See *also*
World, Flesh, and the Devil
Lust-liking: character in *Castle
of Perseverance*, 30, 37
Lydgate, John: poet-monk of Bury
St. Edmunds Abbey, 4

Macro, Rev. Cox (1683–1737):
owner of manuscript of *Castle
of Perseverance*, *Mankind*, and
Wisdom, 3; born at Bury, 133n16
Macro plays: owners of, 2–3;
moral instruction in, 4; style of,
5; folio 191 of, 40; as celebrations, 119–20; artistry mirrors
medieval view of cosmos, 128;
mentioned, xiv. See *also Castle
of Perseverance; Mankind;
Wisdom*
Maintenance: character in *Wisdom*, 102
Malice: character in *Wisdom*, 102
Mankind: at center of morality
plays, 1
Mankind: as religious allegory,
xiii; written ca. 1467, 2; first
modern performance, 3; called
"theologically ignorant," 5;
Mercy as dominant character,
22; plot summary, 65–65; discussed, 64–93; stylistic ornaments, 65–69; hero's profession,
69; realistic elements, 69–77;
characterizations, 72–77; production requirements, 77–81;
informal production, 78–80; audience, 78–82; plot sequence,
82, 90–92; illustrated sermon as
organizing principle, 83–90; pattern of alternation, 91–93, 124;
similarities to other plays, 121;
unified by design, 123; performance in Lent, 140n7; mentioned,
4, 24, 27, 94, 104
Mankind (character): saved by
Mercy, 26; in *Castle of Perseverance*, 29, 30, 33–34, 41–60
passim; costume, 36–37; in
Mankind, 64–65, 67; diction
mirrors spiritual state, 68; as
hero is representative of all
men, 69–70; characterization
shifts, 75–76; actions in play
controlled by doctrine, 77;
farmer's costume, 80; entrance,
84; actions fit play design,
85–87; inconstancy, 88; alternating nature, 92–93; in *Wisdom*, 94; presented in nine
parts, 107; mentioned, 23, 24,
71–74, 78, 83, 89
Masque, paraliturgical: genre of
Wisdom, 104–5, 144n7
Mathematical: symmetry of allegory in *Wisdom*, 107–18. See

156

Index

Mankind reminiscent of, 85
Mundus et Infans (ca. 1520), 2
Mystery play cycles: as mixtures of elements, 122; mentioned, 1

Narrative patterning: types in medieval literature, 127
Newguise, Nowadays, and Nought: characters in *Mankind*, 23, 64–65, 69–71; stanza pattern, 67; individuals, not concepts, 72; motivation within play, 77; costumes, 80, 81–92 passim; mentioned, 73, 78
New Testament. *See* Evangelists, Four
Nine-part composite: of human soul in *Wisdom*, 94, 107, 109–10, 115, 118
Nine points pleasing to God: in *Wisdom*, 114
Nominalists, 27
Norfolk: handwriting style of *Castle of Perseverance*, 3, 132n15
Nought. *See* Newguise, Nowadays, and Nought
Nowadays. *See* Newguise, Nowadays, and Nought
Number as design: in *Wisdom*, 106–18. *See also* Design; Ornamentation; Principle of organization

Organization. *See* Principle of organization
Orléans, Lorens d': author of *Somme des Vices et des Vertues*, 21
Ornamentation: stylistic, 8–18

passim, 22, 25; in *Castle of Perseverance*, 32, 38–54, 56, 62; in *Mankind*, 65–69, 77, 91, 92; in *Wisdom*, 96–101 passim, 121. *See also* Design; High style elements; Realism
Outdoor performance: in *Castle of Perseverance*, 30

Parallels: of three-part sequences in *Wisdom*, 116, 118. *See also* Angels
Parlement of Foules. *See* Chaucer, Geoffrey
Parody: and contrast in *Mankind*, 90, 93; in *Wisdom*, 102
Particularity: form of decorative realism in *Castle of Perseverance*, 32, 35; in *Mankind*, 70, 75–76, 92; in *Wisdom*, 101–3. *See also* Realism
Patience: character in *Castle of Perseverance*, 29, 49–50. *See also* Virtues
Peace. *See* Daughters of God, Four
Pearl Poet, 120
Penitence: as theme in Macro plays, 28; as characters in *Castle of Perseverance*, 47
Penitential works: in fourteenth and fifteenth centuries, 21
Perceptual example: combined with allegory in flamboyant style, 12. *See also* Realism
Perceptual realism. *See* Particularity; Realism
Personification: as decoration, 9.
Piers Plowman (fourteenth century), 22

Index

scheme in *Mankind*, 67; in *Wisdom*, 100; signals three-part divisions in *Wisdom*, 116, 118
Robbery: character in *Wisdom*, 102
Roman de la Rose, Le, 13
Royal Book: by William Caxton, 21

Scenery: scaffolds in *Castle of Perseverance*, 32, 36; used sparingly in *Mankind*, 78; none in *Wisdom*, 105. *See also* Production requirements; Stage
Scholastic philosophy: as artists' example, 125
Sens Cathedral: rose window as example of flamboyant style, 7, 8
Seven Cardinal Virtues, 21. *See also* Virtues
Seven Deadly Sins: in *Castle of Perseverance*, 29, 46; as dancers in *Wisdom*, 102–3; twenty-one aspects in *Wisdom*, 113; mentioned, 11, 12. *See also* Anger; Avarice; Envy; Gluttony; Lechery; Pride; Sloth
Sermon: commonplaces reflected in morality plays, 25; with illustrative dramatizations in *Mankind*, 71; as organizing principle in *Mankind*, 88–89
Sharp, Thomas: printed stage plan of *Castle of Perseverance* in 1823, 3
Similarities: in structure of Macro plays, 121
Sins, three major: in *Wisdom*, 111; antitheses of religious

vows, 111. *See also* Covetousness; Lechery; Pride
Sleight: character in *Wisdom*, 102
Sloth: character in *Castle of Perseverance*, 35–37, 47; mentioned, 103. *See also* Seven Deadly Sins
Small Crucifixion, The. See Grünewald, Mathis
Somme des Vices et des Vertues. See Orléans, Lorens d'
Sound structure: as ornament in *Castle of Perseverance*, 42; adjusted to characterization in *Mankind*, 67; in *Wisdom*, 116. *See also* Meter; Rhyme
Spectacle. *See* Dramatic spectacle
Stage: plan of *Castle of Perseverance*, 3, 31, 32, 36; set in *Mankind*, 78. *See also* Production requirements; Scenery
Stanza: arrangement of rhyme, meter, and meaning in *Castle of Perseverance*, 38–54; patterns of balanced symmetry, 43; in *Mankind*, 67; ornamental form in *Wisdom*, 100
Structural: component, xiv; signaling in *Castle of Perseverance*, 57; patterns in *Wisdom*, organized by number three, 96, 106, 112–13, 116–18; reality of medieval art, 123. *See also* Design; Principle of organization
Structure of sound. *See* Sound structure
Sturdiness: character in *Wisdom*, 102
Stylistic features: as formal ele-